CHRISTIAN FEMINISM

By the Same Editor

Women Ministers

CHRISTIAN FEMINISM
Visions of a New Humanity

Edited by Judith L. Weidman

HARPER & ROW, PUBLISHERS, SAN FRANCISCO
Cambridge, Hagerstown, New York, Philadelphia
London, Mexico City, São Paulo, Sydney

FIRST EDITION

Library of Congress Cataloging in Publication Data
Main entry under title:

CHRISTIAN FEMINISM.

  Includes bibliographical references
  1. Woman (Christian theology)—Addresses, essays, lectures.   2. Feminism—Religious aspects—Christianity—Addresses, essays, lectures.   I. Weidman, Judith L.
BT704.C48   1984   261.8′344   83–48462
ISBN 0–06–069292–8

84 85 86 87 88 10 9 8 7 6 5 4 3 2 1

Contents

Introduction

JUDITH L. WEIDMAN

"The more one becomes a feminist, the more difficult it becomes to go to church."

That is said by many women these days, but not all succumb to the difficulty. This is a book by Christian women who are still "hanging in" with the church. They come from academia—some well-established names and some "comers"—and from national and international agencies of the church. Their writings belie their varied contexts and agendas, but together they are helping to shape the church and society in our time.

In one sense feminist theologians are playing a bit of catchup in the culture. When the current women's movement surfaced in the sixties, it was primarily a white, middle-class reaction of bored suburban housewives.[1] Its concern for full personhood, while spiritual in scope, did not emerge from the church, nor was it a major force in the church until more than a decade later. And it has taken most of another decade for the development of systematic work by feminist theologians and ethicists.

This book draws together a sampling of that work. The authors recapitulate some of the now familiar critiques of patriarchy, which paint Christianity as a sexist religion in which a male God and an overwhelming tradition of male leadership give credence to the superiority of men in the family and society. But these authors move on quickly to suggest the work yet to be done in the next round of scholarship.

Judith L. Weidman, associate general secretary of interpretation of the United Methodist Board of Higher Education and Ministry, is an ordained clergywoman in the United Methodist Church. She writes frequently for denominational and ecumenical publications and is the author of a study unit for women in prison and the editor of *Women Ministers: How Women Are Redefining Traditional Roles.*

Ours is a turbulent time, a time of creation. Feminists have taken a clue from black theology, and they draw on liberation theologies; but what is most exciting is that they are calling into question the full range of human relationships and church life and practice. Feminist theology is not a theology solely about women; it has taken on the whole of humanity, and it touches on every contemporary issue.[2]

The contributors to this book hang in with the church because they believe that it bears the seeds of its own renewal. As Nanette Roberts notes, our hope is in "reforming our faith by our faith." And these feminists believe that the church is *worth* reforming. Despite its decline in the culture, it is still a locus of expectation for many persons. Beverly Harrison, addressing a national consultation of United Methodist clergywomen, suggests that the church is a critical arena because it is one of the few institutions in our society to which people still turn with any expectation of sustenance for their basic humanity.[3]

Christian feminism is by definition a phenomenon that arises out of community, so in many respects the church never had a better friend. Christian feminists have, in fact, dealt privatistic religion a major setback. Feminists begin with the telling and hearing of each other's stories.[4] This nourishes and mobilizes us; it also provides the basis for our theology. Most liberal theologies begin with experience. Feminist theology fills in the missing part—*women's* experience.

The unifying theme of this volume, then, is community. Although Letty Russell acknowledges that community is sometimes "inefficient and messy," the writers without exception hold out for the strength and wisdom that arise when women band together. Elisabeth Fiorenza talks about the "church of women," where visions for change and liberation are ritualized. Rosemary Ruether points to "feminist base communities" as supplementary points of contact for women where personhood, rather than the past accumulation of tradition, is normative. Rita Brock talks about "the healing vision feminism offers from our experience of sisterhood, from the community of women who hear and understand us."

The glory—and ultimately the threat—of this and other

contemporary movements is that our entire society is being re-scripted. Many persons correctly perceive that the women's movement has a major part in the play. Once you begin to un-ravel the dominance of patriarchy, you are left without a defense for everything from clericalism in the church to apartheid in South Africa. And, as we've noted, Christianity not only reflects this male-dominated, hierarchical world-view, it also contributes to it and offers it justification in the culture. Thus feminists support the church at great price.

The issue of Christian feminism is not new. In a sermon deliv-ered in 1893, Anna Howard Shaw observed that "unless woman-hood is developed, one-half of divinity itself is kept from the knowledge of the peoples of the world."

So why have feminist concerns blossomed anew in the culture? Nanette Roberts notes that the liberation of women is being articulated and debated in virtually every arena of our culture—social, political, and religious—and suggests that the basis for this lies in the realms of economic and technological change (es-pecially as it has increased job possibilities), the Pill, and abor-tion. Few remain to be convinced that the resulting life-style changes in our time are fraught with revolutionary potential. With the additional help of Clare Fischer and Connie Parvey, we begin to see that the accompanying human aspirations for equal-ity are affecting the identity and roles of women around the world. Beverly Harrison observes that women's discoveries re-lated to sexuality—seeing ourselves as embodied, psychosexual, spiritual beings—provide a new source of courage and activism.

But this is a time when women are both better off and worse off. Increased visibility, greater self-awareness, more legal sup-port, and expanded vocational opportunities are some of the pluses. There is also evidence, however, of increased rape, do-mestic violence, sexual harassment and intimidation.[5] A lot of people—women and men—are angry and confused. And it's not clear where it's all going to come out.

While strongly critiquing virtually every aspect of Christian life and practice—in fact, indicting it for many social ills—the authors in this volume remain within the tradition. "House revo-lutionaries," you might call them. This is never more evident than in Connie Parvey's reminder that conversion is the church's internal healing and reforming mechanism. She asks, "How can healing take place unless we touch the fire?"

It hasn't been easy to get the church's attention on feminist issues. All that suddenly changed, however, with the language issue.[6] It is precisely that issue which is currently bringing the feminist agenda to the church's attention most forcefully. Marjorie Suchocki has suggested in a journal article that the threat which occurs when religious symbols undergo change is a threat to the means whereby a person can accept and integrate change. Thus change in liturgy, ritual, or church office meets with an intensity of resistance that can only be attributed to the felt need for stability and order.[7]

The rallying point for countless letters to church agencies has been the concern, "You're rewriting the Bible." The urgency of the need for reform was all the more evident when it became obvious that persons who have called God "father" and "king" and "Lord" all their lives really think of God as a male person. The problem, then, is theological (how we image God) as well as sociological (what happens to women when "male" is normative). These concerns permeate both sections of the book.

The overriding issue, of course, is change—change in church life and practice as well as cultural norms. Pollster Daniel Yankelovich reminds us that nothing of enduring cultural value is born without struggle. Culture, he says, evolves in indirect, dialectical fashion. This is the process: An idea is introduced and initially rejected by those whose interests are threatened. But once planted, the idea takes root and begins to sprout in a variety of forms. Inevitably, a second wave of resistance arises, but by then the new idea is able to advance by forcing adjustments in the culture. By the time the new idea has triumphed, it claims many mothers and fathers.[8]

I believe this to be the case in the women's movement as well. The implications of feminist concerns for theological reconstruction and the church's social ministry are staggering. New dialogue is now under way because of the struggle of women for self-definition in our time. The vision spelled out in these chapters is of a community of women and men that celebrates the

distinctiveness of each person, male and female, while supporting new patterns of independence and reciprocity. We take a
clue from Habakkuk:

> Write the vision;
>> make it plain upon tablets,
>> so [they] may run who read it.
> For still the vision awaits its time;
>> it hastens to the end—it will not lie.
> If it seems slow, wait for it;
>> it will surely come, it will not delay.
>
>>>> —Hab. 2:2–3

I. CHURCH LIFE AND PRACTICE

1. Feminist Theology and Spirituality

ROSEMARY RADFORD RUETHER

WHAT IS THEOLOGY; WHAT IS FEMINIST THEOLOGY?

I would define theology as reflection on human experience in the light of our relation to God. By "God" I mean the transcendent matrix of Being that underlies and supports both our own existence and our continual potential for new being. This relation to God provides humanity with its authentic ground and potential (*imago dei*) over against the historical deformation of that potential by egoism, fear, and self-alienation which give rise to systematic structures of social alienation and oppression: sexism, racism, classism, and so on. Human experience of self-discovery and transformation thus exists in dialectical relationship with this historic reality of alienation and oppression (sin, fallenness).

The need for feminist theology arises from the historical reality of sexism in human societies. Sexism as an expression of broken mutuality between the genders, the subjugation of women to men, arises at an early period of human development and becomes accentuated and ideologically hardened in the processes that led to historical civilizations. Sexism results in the exclusion of women from social development in the valued sphere of cul-

Rosemary Radford Ruether is the Georgia Harkness Professor of Applied Theology at Garrett–Evangelical Theological Seminary and a member of the faculty of the joint program, Northwestern University. She has also taught at Howard University, Harvard, and Yale divinity schools. She is the author of many articles and sixteen books. Her recent books include *Women and Religion in America: A Documentary History* (of which she is co-editor) and *Sexism and God-Talk: Toward a Feminist Theology.*

tural formation and leadership. Religion plays a key role here both in being shaped by and in sacralizing the social patterns of sexism. Religion makes sexism appear the normative nature of human relations, the order of creation, and the relation of God to humanity and history.

The intertwining of sexism with religion means not only that women and women's experience have been excluded from the shaping of the public culture of religion as both theology and cult. It also means that the religious codes, cult, and symbolic patterns, especially in the Judeo-Christian tradition, have been shaped by an ideological bias *against* women. God is imaged as a great Patriarch. Male heads of families, in turn, come to be regarded as the normative representatives of God. Women are regarded as possessing "less" of the image of God than males. They are marginal and nonnormative. They are an "inferior mix" representing the sinful and alien tendencies of human existence, rather than its good potential. Only the male can represent generic humanity, both for himself, and as "head" of the woman. The woman is regarded as more responsible for sin than the male, and thus her historical condition of suppression and exploitation is interpreted as a just punishment for her sin of "getting out of her place," rather than itself as an expression of sin.

In patriarchal theology, woman not only fares badly in the doctrines of God, creation, and sin, but little better in the doctrines of redemption. The redeemer is seen as normatively male, reinforcing the male nature both of God and the imago dei. Woman is saved only by redoubling her humiliation for sin and transcending her female (sexual) nature. Her female nature is regarded as an obstacle to redemption for herself and, even more, for the male. Redemption is seen as a repudiation of the "lower sphere" associated with femaleness, bodiliness, and finitude. Woman cannot represent Christ in the leadership of the church, but only the sinner who is redeemed by him. She is to take a silent and passive role in the church and aspire to a realm of redemption beyond history that will finally neutralize her femaleness and allow her "angelic" equivalence with the male. This, in simplified, but, in no sense, exaggerated terms, has been the dominant line of orthodox Christian theology.

Feminist theology arises at the point where this sexist bias of classical theology is perceived and repudiated. Feminist theology essentially has two interacting movements or agendas. One agenda, and usually the first to be developed, is a critique of the sexist bias of theology itself. This bias is unmasked and named. By implication this sexist bias loses its normative status and claim to represent "truth" and instead is put under judgment. Systematic investigations are carried out to demonstrate the nature and pattern of this sexist bias in various theologians and periods of theology: Biblical, Patristic, Medieval, Reformation, and Modern. Surveys of sexist bias in theology are written, followed by in-depth studies of particular periods and writers. It becomes apparent that this bias is not marginal or accidental, is not the result of idiosyncratic views of a few writers, but runs through the whole tradition and shapes the total structure of theology.

But feminist theology does not stop at this unmasking of sexist bias. Otherwise it would have only a critique of theology, pointing to the rejection of theology itself, rather than a feminist theology. Feminist theology becomes possible only when it is perceived that the basic foundations of theology itself, that is, the reflection on human experience in relation to God, cannot only be rescued from sexist bias, but can be reconstructed as the authentic base from which to critique this sexist bias. Feminist theology starts with the affirmation that God, the ground of being and new being, underlies, includes, supports, and promotes female personhood as much as male personhood. Woman is not subordinate or "included under," but equivalent as imago dei.

In the light of the equivalent personhood of woman, sexism must be evaluated as a fundamental expression of sin, alienation, oppression, and fallenness. The redeeming work of God, the human experience of conversion, transformation, new being, and new community, therefore, must be seen as overcoming this historical alienation and distortion of relationship between men and women. The sexist bias of patriarchal theology, then, must be evaluated as blasphemous ratification of sin in God's name, rather than an authentic expression of liberating knowledge. Feminist theology engages in a systematic reconstruction of all the symbols of human relation to God to delegitimize sexist bias and to manifest an authentic vision of redemption as liberation from sexism.

But if redemption from sexism is the authentic meaning and message of theology, why had this never been seen before? An obvious answer to this lies in the social exclusion of women from the study and teaching of theology. The sexist bias of theology could not be criticized until women themselves gained access to the forums of theology and were able to shape the teaching and preaching of the church. This began to happen very slowly from 1850–1956. Only in the last twenty-five years (and, mostly, in the last ten years) have some women gained access to seminaries, to pulpits, and to theological faculties. Thus it is not surprising that the criticism of the sexist bias of theology only began in the last decade or two.

Yet it is difficult to be satisfied with this answer, because it leaves feminist theology without any tradition at all. Patriarchal theology does provide basic patterns, in biased form, which feminist theology uses as "matter" for transformation. But the normative principle of feminist theology, the full personhood of women, seems to be something that women are left to affirm without roots in past theological tradition. If this is indeed the normative principle for liberating theology from sexist bias, surely this is not the first time in human history that this has been glimpsed! Feminist theology seeks an alternative tradition that can ground its own normative principle in a heritage of human experience.

The search for alternative experience *within* the accepted canons of patriarchal theology yields meager fruit at first. But gradually feminist research begins to widen the limits of this search and to discover many helpful hints. These are found: (a) in the prophetic, critical tradition of biblical thought—unfortunately, this critique of oppression is seldom applied to women as an oppressed group; (b) in mystical and sectarian groups who focus on the reconciliation of the "masculine" and the "feminine," but generally in ways that preserve unsatisfactory dualism of body and spirit; (c) in a few groups, such as Montanists and Quakers, who momentarily touch on the connection between the liberation of the oppressed and the reconciliation of the feminine and the masculine. (But their voices are fragmentary. They seemed to have been either suppressed or co-opted into the dominant system. The momentary promise failed to develop into a cohesive alternative to patriarchal theology.); and (d) in pre-Christian and non-Christian religions that affirm the image of the divine as female as well as male. (But it is not clear what this meant in terms of social equality of women.)

Thus the search for alternative tradition yields a growing and impressive array of bits, pieces, and beginnings, glimpsed between the lines of the history of patriarchal suppression. But the connecting of these together, the systematic transformation of the whole theological pattern in the light of the alternative norm of women's equivalent personhood, the translation of this into transformed preaching, ministry, and community—all seems to await a future that has only just begun. This might be daunting indeed if it were not necessary and inevitable for women, once empowered to do theology, to *believe in* their own equivalent personhood as the normative starting point of theology *more than they can believe in* any past accumulation of tradition which has been carried on without and against women's participation.

WHAT IS FEMINIST SPIRITUALITY?

There are in the North American world at the present moment two primary contenders for the definition of feminist spirituality. These two contenders appear, from the perspective of this writer, to fall into two different patterns, which might be characterized as the "aesthetic" and the "ethical" understandings of feminist theology. The aesthetic position assumes that there is a pre-existing harmony between all parts of reality. Yin and yang, male and female, spirit and flesh, humans and nature, nature and the divine, all are parts of one primal rhythm. The breaking of this harmony into contraries is an illusion. Sin and evil do not really exist. It is a lie foisted upon us by antinatural civilization. One has only to escape from civilization back to nature to reembrace the primal harmony. Rituals and chants disenchant the false world of contraries and put us back in union with the primal harmony.

This primal harmony lies under the sign of the primacy of the mother. The original deity of humanity was the Mother

Goddess, representing this primal rule of the mother. The advent of father rule broke the primal harmony and subjugated the mother. Bliss and harmony will be restored by escaping from father culture in all its forms, especially its religious forms, and reembracing the religious of the Mother Goddess, either as groups of women exclusively or as groups which include males, but only those who accept the integration of maleness *under* mother rule.

This religion of primary harmony under the Mother Goddess is presumed to reflect both the actual religion and the actual sociology of prepatriarchal matriarchal cultures. They correspond to "original paganism" before its distortion by patriarchy and suppression by Judaism, Christianity, and Islam. Feminist religion necessarily involves a root and branch repudiation of biblical religion in favor of goddess religion.

The "ethical" or "liberation" perspective on feminist theology also believes in original harmony as a symbol of the authentic ground and potential of human life. But it takes more seriously the broken relations between self and body, self and others, self and nature, self and God, as creating not just false images, but also broken and distorted existence. It sees this brokenness as generating a massive historical counterreality, a system of evil relationships that divides all reality from its authentic potential. This corruption does not leave either side uncorrupted. One cannot imagine that maleness and fathering stand for falsehood, but femaleness and motherhood stand for unbroken harmony; that civilization stands for corruption, but uncultivated nature stands for unbroken harmony; that reason is distorted, but spontaneous bodily appetites connect us with harmony and goodness.

If patriarchal theology sacralized the lie of distorted relations by making the male side of the dualism good and the female evil, goddess religion is in danger of simply reversing the same dualisms. Liberation feminism does not believe that one can banish the contradictions by cultural methods of identifying with the maternal pole against the paternal pole of the traditional dualism. Rather, it calls for an ethical struggle to transform both the self and the social system that supports exploitative relations. Females as well as males, nature as well as civilization, bodiliness as well as rationality, have been distorted by sinful existence.

Both sides need to be transformed into a new whole.

Liberation feminist spirituality finds this tradition of critical judgment and transformation at the base of the Jewish and Christian prophetic tradition. It cannot deny that it learned this pattern of thought from biblical religion and that biblical religion taught this tradition to modern liberation movements. Thus while it repudiates the patriarchy of biblical religion, it nevertheless claims this underlying prophetic base of biblical religion. Feminist theology should not fall back on biblical exclusivism over against "paganism." It should not call for biblical religion as the "true" foundation of feminism over against non-Christian traditions. Rather it should raise questions about all religious exclusivism, including the reversed use of exclusivism by goddess religion to repudiate biblical religion.

Many of the theses of goddess religion are problematic. It is not clear that female symbols of God point to original matriarchy. Moreover, it does not appear that the joint worship of gods and goddesses in ancient cultures represented the dualisms of the feminine against the masculine, nature against civilization. These are modern dualisms generated by post-Christian culture out of and against inherited Christian patterns. Indeed what may be a positive resource of ancient paganism is that both male and female symbols of the divine represented divine sovereignty in a way that united natural and social powers.

Feminist theology seeks to transcend the dichotomy of biblical exclusivism or a reversed exclusivism that would call for the rejection of biblical religion in favor of a "goddess religion." Instead, it should seek to recapitulate the religious journey of the Near Eastern, Mediterranean, and Western worlds in a way that could embrace both non-Christian and Christian traditions, both suppressed and dominant traditions—in Mary Wakeman's words, "By reaching back and encompassing, we point forward to a new synthesis."[1]

The feminist religious perspective that seems, to this author, most helpful is one that draws on a liberation theology perspective. This perspective does not exclude the invoking of religious symbols from outside the biblical tradition, as well as from suppressed traditions that have been condemned as "heretical." But it draws in this larger heritage through the liberation theology perspective, rather than from a perspective that opts for one side (maternal, natural, pagan) against the other (paternal, historical, biblical). It seeks to get to the root alienation behind these dualisms, expressed in exploitative social patterns, to create a new humanity and new social relations beyond these divisions.

DIRECTIONS FOR THE FEMINIST RECONSTRUCTION OF THEOLOGICAL SYMBOLS

We have said that feminist theology must engage in a systematic reconstruction of all the religious symbols of the human-God relationship to delegitimize sexist bias and to manifest the authentic vision of redemption as a liberation from sexism. I would like to illustrate briefly what this might mean in terms of several key symbols: God-language, cosmology or creation, Christology, anthropology, and redemption. Then I will try to sketch what the actual spirituality and practice of such a liberation feminism might mean in terms of the ministry and community of the church.

GOD-LANGUAGE

If we are to seek an image of God beyond patriarchy, certain basic principles have to be acknowledged. First, we have to acknowledge the principle that the male has no special priority in imaging God. Christian theology has always recognized, theoretically, that all language for God is analogical or metaphorical, not literal. No particular image can be regarded as the exclusive image for God. Images for God must be drawn from the whole range of human experience, from both genders, and all social classes and cultures. To take one image drawn from one gender and in one sociological context (that of the ruling class) as normative for God is to legitimate this gender and social group as the normative possessors of the image of God and representatives of God on earth. This is idolatry. It is to make the image of God a sanction of evil and injustice. Thus the recognition that all God-language is analogical must lead us to the further recognition that language for God must be gender inclusive. Images drawn from women's roles are as appropriate as those drawn for male roles.

Language for God as either mother or father is based on the fundamental analog of God to parents. This is natural and understandable. Our parents are the immediate source of our being. So parent language is analogous to God as the ultimate source of our being. But even parent language must be recognized as a limited image for God. It does not exhaust the way we should image our relationship to God. Overreliance on parental imagery for God suggests that we should relate to God primarily in the mode of childlike dependency. When this mode of relationship is made the primary language for God, it promotes spiritual infantilism and cuts off moral maturity and responsibility. God becomes the neurotic parent who wishes us to remain always dependent children and is angry with us when we want to grow up. Thus we must balance the language of God as parent with other images, such as God as teacher, guide, and liberator. We need to see the dynamic relationship between God as the source of our being and God as the empowerer of our aspiration and growth toward new being, toward redeemed and fulfilled humanity.

Theologies of hope or of liberation affirm the God of history, the God of Exodus who liberates us from slavery and leads us to the promised land of future wholeness and goodness. But the language of God as liberator, in a patriarchal context, has been typically imaged as a rejection of the God of nature, of God as ground of being or creation. Such a concept of God as liberator in rejection of nature makes the fundamental mistake of identifying the ground of nature or creation with the foundations and legitimization of existing social systems. Being, matter, or nature is seen as the ontological foundations of "what is." Since "what is," socially and historically, is corrupt and evil, immanentist language of God is seen as sanctifying social systems of evil. The theology of hope sees a dualism between nature and spirit, creation and redemption.

Feminist theology must reject this dualism of nature and spirit, or immanence and transcendence. It must reject both the image of static immanence, tied to existing social systems, and also the ideal of spirit and transcendence as rootless, antinatural, originating in another world beyond the cosmos, ever repudiating and fleeing from nature, body, and the visible world. Feminist theology affirms the God of Exodus, God as liberator, but as rooted in the foundations of being rather than as its antithesis. The God (or perhaps we should say God-ess) is the foundation of both our being and our new being. Holy Wisdom embraces both the ground of the substratum of our existence (matter) and its endlessly new potential (spirit). The Holy Wisdom who is the foundation of our being/new being does not confine us to a stifled, dependent self nor uproot us into a spirit trip outside the earth. Rather he/she leads us to the converted center, the harmonization of self and body, self and other, self and world. She/he is the *shalom* of our being.

COSMOLOGY/CREATION

There are two basic models of nature or creation that have shaped Western Christian imagination. The first is that of nature as a hierarchy or "great chain of being." The second model is that of historical transcendence or progressivism by which humanity evolves or develops toward perfection historically. This idea of growth toward perfection within history is based on the messianic vision. It can be seen in either an evolutionary or a revolutionary way, that is, as continuous growth based on creation as "good" but immature, or a series of transformations or conversions in which evil is defeated and good installed as a new possibility on earth. In any case, redemption is seen as the ultimate end of a historical process.

Both of these models have lent themselves to ideologies of social bigotry toward others. In the great chain of being, God is seen as the apex of the system. "He" is Pure Spirit. Cosmology is seen as "trickling down" from God as Pure Spirit to a bottom point of "pure matter." In between are various gradations of matter and spirit: angels, humans, animals, plants, rocks. Each level above is both morally and ontologically superior to that below it and is mandated to rule over it. God rules over the whole, and angels rule the cosmos as delegates of God. Humans, in turn, rule over the natural order.

Within the human community also there is an analogous hierarchy. Men rule over women, masters over slaves, whites over blacks, just as God rules nature, head rules body and "man" rules the natural order "beneath him." Thus the great chain of being mandates both the social hierarchy of ruling-class males over others and the hierarchy of "man" over nature (exercised, in practice, by ruling-class males).

The evolutionary or revolutionary models of history as movement toward perfection are ones that have particularly captured Western imagination in the last two hundred years. They suppose, paradoxically, that a process of infinite expansion within history can culminate within history in a point of completion or final perfection. This viewpoint leads to several contradictions. Either the final endpoint escapes out of history altogether to some transcendence beyond history so history itself is seen as leading nowhere and ceasing to be a medium of hope for a better future, or else it leads to the mythical pursuit of the revolution that never comes. If the final endpoint is identified with a particular revolution, this then absolutizes that particular revolution and tends to make it totalitarian and intolerant toward further criticism.

The model of history as progress also tends to assume that certain peoples or groups are the favored agents of historical progress. Males, Protestant Christians, and Anglo-Saxons lead the march of progress. Jews, Indians, Catholics, and other such people, represent a "retarded" humanity that is to be left behind or exterminated by the triumphal march of the Spirit. Or else, in reverse of this, oppressed people such as the proletariat will defeat the evil oppressors on the historical stage and inherit the earth. The former owners will be defeated and wither away. Messianism becomes a theology of revenge to be vindicated historically.

Feminist theology must question both these models of nature and the human-nature relationship. There is no final point of perfection to be reached within history through infinite growth or final revolution. To be alive is to be engaged in endless process and change. This does not mean that change goes "nowhere" or that history is just "one damn thing after another," but we must reimage our model of historical change in a way more consonant with the realities of finitude. There are certain ingredients of a just and livable society. Such a just and livable society must be based on just relationships between all persons and harmonious relationships with the environment. Change must be seen in the mode of continuous *conversion* to this center of just, livable relationships. It is a continuous renewal that is, at the same time, restoration of balance and harmony, in correction of the constant tendency of humans to drift into distorted relationships with nature and each other. Change as conversion back to the center is not simply repetition or "cyclical change," for it must take new forms in each new historical context. Yet it is always rediscovery, in new contexts, of basic truths, the truths of our authentic existence.

Likewise, the relation of humanity and nature, God and nature, is not to be seen on the model of a hierarchy of mind or body, ruler over ruled. Rather, we should see our relationships to nature and to each other as a mutuality of gifts and services. We both give to and receive from all around us in a way that our very giving is not impoverishing but enriching. Nonhuman nature is not something "beneath us," as a reality of lesser status and value which we are to rule over. Nature does not need us to rule over it. It gets along very well—in fact, better—without us. It runs by its own immanent laws and balances.

Humans have intervened in nature too often to distort these balances and create pollution and waste. We must learn to use the gift of intelligence as servant rather than master of nature, to refine and sustain those processes by which nature renews itself, renews its own life processes, and generates an infinite variety of creatures. Only by making human intelligence the expression of a "good gardener," rather than a destroyer and exploiter, can we learn to live in harmony with nature as friend of the earth, helping to sustain and enhance those processes of life renewal for the sake both of our progeny and of all earth's creatures.

CHRISTOLOGY

Christology is the doctrine that should sum up our hopes for a redeemed humanity. In Christ one should see both a paradigm and an empowerment to create this redeemed humanity. Yet, ironically, Christology has become the doctrine of the Christian tradition most used against women. The maleness of Jesus is used to suggest that men alone can represent Christ in the priesthood. Women are redeemed by but, somehow, cannot image

Christ. This translation of Christology into a ratification of male domination comes about through the transposition of the reality of Christ from the future that is in the process of being revealed to a cosmological doctrine of the great chain of being. The Logos or Word of God is seen as the rule of this top-down cosmology. Males, in turn, are seen as expressing, in the human order, the domination of spirit over nature, mind over body.

A feminist Christology must restore the understanding of Christ to its true function as paradigm of the liberated humanity that comes to us from a still unrealized future, rather than justifying patriarchal and hierarchical social systems through a sacral cosmology of the status quo. First and most obviously, feminist Christology must stress that the incarnation is inclusive of all human beings of all races and historical conditions and both genders. The historical accidents of Jesus' person—maleness, Jewishness, social class—do not suggest that God is more incarnate into these particularities than into others. This has always been clear in terms of ethnic and social identity.

However, Christians have, falsely, used Jesus' gender to suggest that maleness is more appropriate to God than femaleness, and so, in some way, the male better represents Christ than the female. It is impossible, theologically, to vindicate this view without rejecting the universality of the incarnation and making it an exclusive doctrine that redeems only those like Jesus in these particularities, rather than those unlike him. The historical particularities of Jesus' person only make clear that all persons exist in historical particularities. But the significance of the incarnation lies in the ability of this person to stand for us all, to be paradigmatic of human nature and the human condition generically. The humanity into which the Word is incarnated is inclusive of men and women, all races and social conditions.

But, still further, feminist Christology must free the doctrine of Christ from that cosmology which ratifies the status quo. The social praxis by which God's prophetic word reveals itself in Jesus is one in which God comes in judgment on oppressive and unjust social systems. God's prophet demythologizes those religious ideologies that justify such oppressive systems as the will of God. Instead, the will of God is revealed as one that is putting down the mighty from their thrones and lifting up the oppressed. God's Word comes as a transforming power in history that overthrows distorted systems and restores God's shalom or God's kingdom as the place where God's will is done on earth. This means that God's prophetic word does not come to ratify male domination but to overturn it, to raise up women from their subjugated position and to lead all humanity, both men and women, into that pleasant plain where we can live in peace and harmony with each other. Thus Christology must be rediscovered as the doctrine of God as liberator and humanity as liberated.

Finally, we must overcome that closed model of Christology which makes the person of Jesus, as a past historical figure, the sole and exclusive model of Christ. Jesus must be seen as paradigmatic of the redeemed humanity in his faithfulness to God's will, even to death. He is an exponent of God's Word, in his critique of oppressive structures and in his announcement of the kingdom. But, that which he announces is not himself, but the liberated humanity to come. It is we, the community of Christ, who must carry on that prophetic denunciation and annunciation and attempt to continue to model, in our converted humanity, that aspiration. That means that, here and now, we encounter Christ not only in the past Jesus, but in our sisters (and brothers) today as well.

ANTHROPOLOGY

Central to feminism is a re-imaged doctrine of anthropology, or, specifically, the revision of the symbology of male and female and their relation to each other. Humanity has always seen, in the division of humans into gender, male and female, a basic symbolism of the dialectics of human existence. But this symbology of humanity as male and female has primarily been done from a male point of view and has been used to ratify the subordinate or auxiliary status of the female in relation to the male. There are two main patterns of gender symbolism in patriarchal theology—the hierarchical model and the complementary model. In the hierarchical model, the male is seen as both the symbol of and the better exponent of the qualities of mind, spirit, and will over the body, the passions. The female represents that which is to be dominated in the self. Her place in the order of creation is to be the obedient servant and follower of the male leadership.

Since the eighteenth century this hierarchical model has gradually been transmuted into a complementary one. The social basis for this change is too complicated to go into here and has been developed at length in other places in this author's writings. Suffice it to say, it has something to do with the secularization of public society and the privatization of religion and the shift in women's roles to more intensive domestication with the loss of productive functions in the home. Thus religion and "femininity" come to be identified with each other by seeing both as expressed by a nonrational spirituality, emotional nurturance, and an ethical stance of altruism and self-sacrifice. There then arises a new dualism and complementarity of masculine and feminine that expresses this home/work, female/male and religious/secular split. Femininity comes to be seen as passive, altruistic, nurturing, and religious. Masculinity as aggressive, egoistic, materialistic, rational, and secular. Males and females are enjoined to find their completion by their relationship to each other in idealized heterosexual union.

All feminists reject the first model of male-female relations as a hierarchical one of domination and subordination. But feminists have been more confused and conflicted about the second model of complementarity. Most recognize that, in its patriarchal form, the complementary model is intended to make women different and, even, better in order to keep her in her place in the home. However idealized, the feminine here is a powerless and auxiliary principle to male ego development. But feminists generally do not simply want to reject the concept of femininity as an inferior expression of humanity and embrace the male model of humanity as self-centered and aggressive. They recognize that, however domesticated and marginalized, those qualities assigned to the female, in fact, represent the better human qualities, those qualities more conducive to peace, love, and caring relationships.

Radical feminists have tended to convert the patriarchal model of complementarity into a feminist version of this dualism. According to these feminists, the female is the more naturally holistic and self-integrated representative of the human species. Women, therefore, seek for holistic and mutual models of relationships, rather than hierarchical or dualistic models. In women there is both reason and feeling, mind and body, self-relatedness and other-relatedness, in a more balanced and mutually enhancing way. Woman is more loving, nurturing, concerned with other and the care of the earth, not simply in a sacrificial way, but in a way that recognizes that this is also the way to become a happy and whole self.

The male, by contrast, is schizophrenic and conflictual. He splits his reason from his feeling, his mind from his body. He suppresses the affective side of himself and projects it on others and calls it his "feminine side." He seeks to dominate others and, at the same time, seeks to co-opt others into servicing those sides of himself that he has suppressed. These tendencies to repression and projection lead to antagonism toward others and toward nature, expressed in racism, sexism, violence, war, and ecological devastation. The male is the rogue elephant of humanity. He is the fallen one. Woman is still in Eden herself, although her external circumstances have been turned into hell.

This feminist version of opposition between male and female is very attractive to feminists. But it lends itself to an ideology of female moral superiority. Women are seen as more naturally good; men more naturally evil. One feels a partial truth in this picture. Woman, precisely in her exclusion from power relationships of domination and her cultivation of service roles, develops those qualities that are necessary, not only to balance, but to transform the distorted tendencies that appear in those who exercise power. But this does not mean that woman is without sin. She has been truncated and distorted through denial of education and expansive opportunities for personal development and self-esteem. She uses the little sphere to which she is confined for manipulative forms of secondary power. Given an opportunity for enlarged power, she too can be as blind and egotistical as any other ruler. The world is not suddenly transformed into Eden because Margaret Thatcher is prime minister.

The destructive patterns of repression and projection are capacities of human personality distortion that are reflected in men or women in relationships or unjust domination and privilege. Those who have been the underside of this process may have been preserved from some aspects of this personality distortion, but they have suffered from others kinds of personality distortion that reflect their diminished sense of self-worth and cultural development. All of us, both men and women, oppressor and oppressed, need to be converted, in somewhat different ways, to that whole humanity which has been denied to us by systems of alienation and social oppression. This fuller humanity demands not only a conversion of the self into its fuller possibilities, but a conversion of society, a transformation of those social structures that set people in opposition to each other. We seek a new social order, a new order of human-nature relations, that both mandates and incarnates mutuality.

REDEMPTION

There is, currently, a deep split among Christians between those who believe that redemption refers to a purely personal, inward, and otherworldly transformation of the self and those who believe that redemption must be social and systemic and refer to a new humanity in a just and peaceful society on earth. Those with a privatized and otherworldly view of redemption accuse the second group of being merely political and unreligious, while the second group claims that the first uses redemption to split self and society, self and creation, in an unbiblical way. The privatized view of sin and salvation ignores the social, historical contexts of evil and fails to take God seriously as creator and redeemer of the world. Such privatized concepts of redemption make conversion an expression of human alienation and reinforce the status quo of injustice.

Feminist theology would agree with this basic critique of privatized views of sin and redemption, except that it would stress the dynamic interconnection of the personal and the social. We cannot split a spiritual, antisocial redemption from the human being as a social being, embedded in socio-political and ecological systems. But neither can we imagine a reconstructed social order without converted selves. Feminism recognizes sinfulness as an expression of precisely this splitting and deformation of our true relationships with all the networks of being with which we are connected.

The quest for the good self and the quest for the good society exist in unbreakable dialectic. One cannot assume with the social managers, whether liberal or socialist, that reorganized social relations on a structural level will automatically produce the new humanity. But one also cannot suppose that simply building up an aggregate of converted individuals will cause them to act differently, and so society will be redeemed without any attention to the structures of power. This has been the delusion of evangelicalism.

Social and historical structures of evil build up a quasi-autonomous life of their own that holds us in bondage as individuals. Yet we are still free. We can begin to act differently and, in so doing, begin to withdraw support from the evil structures. We must begin to model, in our social relationships, the new world that we seek. Thus a feminist liberation spirituality, while seeking a new, nonsexist social order, cannot neglect the cultivation of new interiority. Nor can it suppose simply that new attitudes on the individual level are enough. We must enter into a process in which the liberated self and the transformation of social systems are interconnected.

The vision of a new humanity and a new society that feminism seeks is one in which the false and alienated dualisms that have been justified by sexism have been dismantled, both psychologically and interpersonally, and in terms of the social structures of family, economics, and relationship to the cosmos and to God. We seek a society that affirms the equal value of all persons as human beings. This assumes a society where this affirmation is reflected in democratic structures of participation in political decisions, in equal access to educational and work opportunities. More than just civil equality, one seeks a society that dismantles sexist and class hierarchies, that restores ownership and management of work to the community of workers as the base unit of economic and political relationships.

Still more, feminism seeks a dismantling of that schism of home and work that divides the female "sphere" from the male "world." We seek a society built on organic community where the processes of child raising, of education, or work, or culture, have been integrated in such a way as to allow both men and women to share both child nurturing and homemaking and also creative activity and decision making in society. Still more, we seek an ecological society where human and nonhuman ecologies have been integrated into a harmonious and mutually supportive whole that, together, can sustain and renew life.

MINISTRY AND COMMUNITY FOR A NEW HUMANITY LIBERATED FROM SEXISM

In this section of the discussion of feminist spirituality, I wish to discuss the meaning of ministry and church. What would ministry and church mean if we really took the good news seriously as liberation from patriarchy?

COMMUNITY, CHURCH

Feminist liberation theology starts with church (liberation community) as the context for discussing questions of ritual, creed, or action. All such questions of ritual or creed are meaningless without a basis in a real community committed to liberation from sexism. If sexism is a root expression of sin, then conversion to God and to authentic selfhood is conversion from sexism. Conversion from sexism means both the freeing of oneself from ideologies and roles of sexism, for both females and males, and also a struggle to liberate social structures from these patterns.

Conversion to a new humanity beyond sexism points toward the entrance into a body of people who share this commitment and support each other in it. Where does one find such a community? The historical Christian churches are all but unusable here. They are deeply committed both to sexist symbolism and sexist social structures. Even slight changes, such as inclusive language, generate great resistance. There are, here and there, local churches of more liberal denominations with women pastors or women members of team ministry. Some of these local churches have adopted feminism as part of their understanding of being church. They seek to reflect this in their language, relationships, and social commitment. This is only possible in denominations of relatively free polity where such local churches do not face constant intervention and coercion from hierarchical structures.

In Roman Catholic local churches this kind of nonsexist community appears impossible at the present time. Some local churches or chaplaincies try to approach nonsexist ways of functioning. But the male clerical system and dependency on hierarchy prevents them from carrying this out in more than token ways. Thus it seems that for most Christians, and for Roman Catholics particularly, there is no alternative but to turn to the creation of feminist base communities as the vehicle for experiencing and shaping a community of liberation from sexism.

The feminist base community is an autonomous, self-gathered community that takes responsibility for reflecting upon, celebrating, and acting in the understanding of liberation as redemption from sexism. Such a community may take on as much or as little of the functions of church as they choose. Such groups may range from consciousness-raising discussion groups to communities that would bring together many functions of worship and social action.

The formation of such feminist base communities does not imply a sectarian rejection of the institutional churches. People who find their primary support in such feminist communities may also participate in various structures of institutional church life, seeking to bring the perspective nurtured in the base community to bear on the larger church. The penetration of at least some parts of the institutional church by a feminist perspective is seen as one of the "fields of mission" of the base community. Precisely as one takes seriously this mission to the institutional church, it becomes essential to have a base in a community that really nurtures growth in full personhood of women and men together, rather than church experiences of alienation and fragmentation.

LEADERSHIP (CLERGY)

Feminist liberation communities must necessarily dismantle clericalism. Clericalism must be recognized as rooted in sexist and hierarchical patterns that are incompatible with feminism. Clericalism by definition monopolizes ministry and sacraments as possessions of an elite (male) caste, and reduces the people to dependency. Feminist liberation communities begin in the reappropriation of expropriated ministry and sacraments back to the people. The community as a whole takes responsibility for ministry and for the development of sacramental expressions of initiation, repentance, and growth in redemptive life.

This does not mean that liberation communities lack a need for leadership. Rather leadership can assume its true functionality once it is liberated from clerical monopoly over ministry, Word, and sacrament. Once it is clear that it is the people as a whole who are the ministering and celebrating people, then those of special gifts and skills can be designated within the body to teach, to organize social projects, to develop liturgy. Leadership is called from within the community rather than imposed upon it from without in a way that deprives the community of its own self-articulation.

RITUAL, CULT, SYMBOLS

Tradition has developed three primary rites: the rite of initiation into redemptive life, the rite of penance from what continues to alienate us from redemptive life, and the rite that combines teaching and reflection on redemptive life with symbols of nourishment and growth in it. In addition, there are many particular rites related to times of the year, particularly the celebration of the birth of the redemptive child and the resurrection from the powers of death and evil. Rites of passage from one state of life to another, crises of contemporary social and political life, and times of special joy or sorrow can also be the focus of community ritual.

For a feminist liberation community, rituals are written and shaped to express the root message of redemption as liberation from sexism. This is not intended to mean an unwelcome harangue or constant nit-picking on sexism. If it takes this form, then the community is not really addressing the issue at all. Rather it must take the form of ever more creative exploration of depth symbols of growth in fuller personal potential and transformed social life as the people in the community experience themselves breaking out of the oppressive structures that have bound their life. Although people of special liturgical gifts, knowledge, and poetic or musical capacities might be asked to take particular responsibility for developing liturgical life, it is important for each member of the community to be involved at one time or another in exploring the symbols of newness of life that are most meaningful to them and shaping liturgical forms that express this experience.

Once the community has freed itself from clerical oppression, it can be free to rediscover the value of special celebration garments, a specially designed space set aside for worship, special modes of communication, ritual gestures, chant, song, that set liturgy aside from ordinary life. This does not mean that liturgy refers to some other reality than ordinary life. But it refers to the depth dimension of transformation of everyday life that then refers us back to ordinary life in a new way. If liturgy is too much collapsed into the style and setting of ordinary life, then this depth dimension is not plumbed, and transformed life is not nurtured.

CREED, CODE

Feminist liberation communities might well develop a basic credal statement in which they express their faith in God as the foundation of redemptive personhood of women and men, their critique of sin as broken relationality, their experience of newness of life, and their hopes for a future world. Such a creed would presuppose a basic understanding of redemption as liberation from sexism. It would not be fixed, but open to continual revision as the community expanded its understanding of what that redemption meant.

Its code might take the form of a regular covenanting together in which certain commitments are spelled out. These might include commitments for a stated period of time to certain social ministries, contributions of money and time to such a project. It also should include some general reflection on commitment to each other in terms of crises of daily life. How does the community understand its responsibility for social ethics of its members? If a wife in a relationship is struggling to enter a new stage of life, if her husband is deeply disturbed by her changed relationship to him, if the children are left without family life by this tension, does the community see that as part of its sphere of responsibility or not?

The community needs to talk through and come to some shared understanding and commitments about the extent to which it invests its private life in the group. Basic housekeeping matters—who takes care of what and for how long—need to be worked through and publicly covenanted upon. Otherwise, a few people get stuck doing all the work that should be more equitably shared. In this sense, every community needs a "rule of life," not as something fixed in stone, but as a livable pattern that they revise on a periodic basis.

ACTION, SOCIAL PRACTICE, LIFE STYLE

A liberation community has both an internal and an external mission. It needs to balance these so that all of its energies do not become expended on its internal development at the expense of the world outside, or all its energies are not so other directed that it neglects its own internal hurts and growth. Its internal ministry is directed toward its own growth in human potential through mutual empowerment. It needs to continually ask itself not only what that means in terms of theological or liturgical expression, but what that means in terms of commitment to each other in the crises of daily life. Does it, for example, decide to develop structures of collective child care, operated by both men and women, to overcome the privatization of child care that isolates women in industrial society? Or does it decide to make this part of its external mission, to develop neighborhood child care groups that include both its members and other neighboring families?

The mission of the community to society is based on a vision of a transformed society beyond all the alienating "isms" of exploitation and alienation. A world without militarism, a world with production and consumption systems in harmony with nature, are as much a part of the vision of redemption beyond sexism as are projects of changed roles between men and women. But this vision must be concretized in some particular projects and commitments.

Projects should be chosen both for their relevance to the people of the community and also for their paradigmatic significance in illuminating the larger problems of oppressive structures. In one case this might mean a battered women's shelter; in another it might mean antinuclear action. But the praxis of a community ought to be focused enough that it can mount a significant engagement on the issue. The community needs to struggle against the pressures of endless fragmentation of energies that end in much talk and little significant action. Sorting out a meaningful union of inward spiritual growth and social praxis amid the overload of stimuli of modern communication is one of the fundamental tasks of a liberation community.

This discussion of a feminist base community describes what it would mean to become church if we were truly free and empowered to do so. In taking some responsibility to communicate this vision and transform some places within the historical churches, the base community does not concede that these institutions are more truly church than they are. On the contrary, whether it be as parish or as base community, we are engaged in the same process, to become church as community of liberation and to cease to be the sacralization of the powers and principalities. Base communities need not regard themselves as better than others. Rather, they should recognize that no part of the church, no part of the world, is liberated until we are all liberated.

Whether we gather in living rooms, warehouses, or church buildings, the marks of the authentic church are the same. The church is where the good news of liberation from sexism is preached, where the Spirit is present to empower us to exodus from patriarchy, where a community committed to the new life of mutuality is being gathered together and nurtured, and where the community is spreading this vision and struggle to others.

2. Emerging Issues in Feminist Biblical Interpretation

ELISABETH SCHÜSSLER FIORENZA

The second letter of John—the only writing of the New Testament addressed to a woman—was written "for the sake of the truth that dwells among us and will be with us forever." Biblical interpretation as theological interpretation is concerned with the divine presence dwelling among the people of God in the past and in the present. Feminist biblical interpretation makes explicit that such divine truth and revelatory presence is also found among women who are the "invisible" part of the people of God. It makes explicit that the receivers and proclaimers of such revelation are not solely men but also women. It thus seeks to interrupt the theological silence and ecclesial invisibility of women so that God's grace and truth may reveal itself among us in its fullness.

The critical rereading of the Bible in a feminist key and from women's perspectives is uncovering lost traditions and correcting mistranslations, peeling away layers of androcentric scholarship, and rediscovering new dimensions of biblical symbols and theological meanings. In Bible study groups, sermons, and seminars women rediscover our biblical heritage, realizing that this heritage is part of our power today. Feminist scholars seek to explore systematically the theological questions and hermeneutical issues raised by women in biblical religion. Such a rediscovery

Elisabeth Schüssler Fiorenza is professor of New Testament studies and theology at the University of Notre Dame and the author of, among other books, *In Memory of Her: A Feminist Theological Reconstruction of Christian Origins.* Through her books and lectures she has emerged as an authority on ministries of women in the church and priesthood in the New Testament. She is the author of numerous articles on exegetical-theological issues and on feminist theology and is active in several groups working on the problems of women in church and theology.

of women's biblical heritage on a popular and academic level is made possible by two basic shifts in how we see the world and reality and in how we see the function of biblical texts and interpretations. Such paradigm shifts are, on the one hand, the shift from an androcentric to a feminist perception of the world and, on the other hand, the shift from an apologetic focus on biblical authority to a feminist articulation of contemporary women's experience and struggle against patriarchal oppression in biblical religion.

FROM AN ANDROCENTRIC TO A FEMINIST INTERPRETIVE FRAMEWORK

The resurgence of the women's movement in the sixties revived not just women's political struggle for civil rights and equal access to academic institutions but also brought forth feminist studies as a new intellectual discipline. In all areas of scientific and intellectual knowledge, courses and research projects have developed that seek to expand our knowledge of women's cultural and historical contributions, as well as to challenge the silence about us in historiography, literature, sociology, and all the human sciences. Such feminist scholarship is compensatory as well as revolutionary. It has inaugurated a scientific revolution that engenders a scholarly paradigm shift from an androcentric—male centered—world view and perspective to an inclusive feminist comprehension of the world, human life, and history.

While androcentric scholarship takes *man* as the paradigm human being, feminist scholarship insists on the reconceptualization of our intellectual frameworks in such a way that they become truly inclusive of all human experience and articulate male experience truth as just one particular experience and perception of reality. Feminist scholarship therefore throws into question our dominant cultural mindset articulated in male generic language, classical texts, scholarly frameworks, and scientific reconstructions that make invisible and marginalize women. This androcentric mindset perpetuates the world view and consciousness that women's experiences and cultural contributions are less valuable, less important, or less significant than men's. Feminist studies challenge male symbolic representations, androcentric language, and the habitual consciousness of two sex classes as a "naturally given" and classificatory fact in our language and thought-world. They point to the interaction between language and society, sexual stereotypes and culture, gender and race, as social constructs and political legitimizations. Sexism, racism, imperialism, and militarism constitute different aspects of the same language of oppression in our society.

However, it must be noted that feminist studies articulate the feminist paradigm in different ways and with the help of varying philosophical perspectives. While liberal scholarship, for example, often seeks to show that women were and are equal to men without critically reflecting on the male-centered framework underlying such an argument, feminists coming from an existentialist or a sociology of knowledge approach use as their main heuristic category androcentrism or phallocentrism. While socialist feminists use as their key analytical category the relationship between social class and gender as determinant of women's condition in society, Third World feminists insist on the relationship between racism, colonialism, and sexism as defining women's oppression and struggle for liberation. Such a variety of emphases and approaches results in different conceptions and frameworks of feminism, women's liberation, and of being human in the world.

Such a diversity in approach and polyphony in feminist intellectual articulations is also found among feminists in biblical religion and feminist theologians. There exists not one feminist theology or *the* feminist theology but many different expressions and articulations of feminist theology. These articulations share not only in the diverse presuppositions and perspectives of feminist studies, but also work within the frameworks of divergent theological perspectives, such as neo-orthodoxy, evangelical theology, liberal theology, liberation theology, process theology, or various confessional theological perspectives. As theological articulations, they are rooted in the ecclesial visions and political situations of the Christian or Jewish communities to whom they are committed.

Yet feminist theologies introduce a radical shift into all forms of traditional theology insofar as they insist that the central commitment and accountability for feminist theologians is not to *the* church as a male institution but to women in the churches, not to *the* tradition as such but to a feminist transformation of Christian traditions, not to *the* Bible on the whole but to the liberating word of God coming to articulation in the biblical writings. Feminist theologians who see our work and ourselves as members of the women's movement in the churches and define our allegiances not just in terms of the women's movement in society and culture, tend to articulate our theology also with respect to the religio-political goals, the spiritual needs, and the communal problems of women in biblical religion. The theological discussions on an inclusive translation of the Bible or on the question of God-language are situated in such a context within organized biblical religion.

Those of us who do not understand ourselves as members of biblical communities, but are committed to the religious quest of women in different cultures and religions, tend to formulate our questions and theological perspectives more in terms of a religious studies approach. In such a history of religions approach, the situation of women in the Bible or in early Christianity is studied as a part of the Oriental or Greco-Roman world and religion to which the biblical writings belong. Such research has had significant results with respect to women in Egypt, Rome, or Judaism and has shattered the apologetic assumption that biblical religion has emancipated ancient women.

Jewish feminists in turn have pointed out that a Jewish feminist biblical interpretation has to wrestle with a different set of theological problems and hermeneutical frameworks than Christian feminist scholarship of the Bible. Not only do Christians claim the New Testament and the Hebrew Bible as their own holy scriptures, but they have also to deal with the anti-Judaism codified in the New Testament. Moreover, Judaism has developed quite distinct exegetical methods and hermeneutical traditions. Finally, insofar as theology as a concept is not as central to Jewish as to Christian thought and life, the very concept of a Jewish feminist theology becomes less important. Therefore we cannot speak about a feminist biblical interpretation as long as Jewish feminist hermeneutics has not developed in its own rights and articulated its own specific questions and approaches. The following must thus clearly be understood as written from a feminist Christian theological perspective. I have defined this perspective as a feminist critical theology of liberation. Such articulation of my own feminist theological perspective has grown out of my experience as a Catholic Christian woman and is indebted to historical-critical scholarship, critical theory, and political as well as liberation theology.

At this point it becomes necessary to explicate my understanding of feminism and of patriarchal oppression. Feminism is not just a theoretical world view or perspective but a women's liberation movement for societal and ecclesial change. Likewise patriarchal oppression is not identical with androcentrism or sexism. It is not just a "dualistic ideology" or androcentric world-construction in language but a social-political system and societal structure of graded subjugations and oppressions. Although this patriarchal system has undergone significant changes throughout its history, it has prevailed as the dominant social-political structure in the last five thousand years or so. Its classical expression is found in Aristotelian philosophy, which has decisively influenced not only Christian theology but also Western culture and political philosophy.[1]

Patriarchy defines not just women as the "other" but it defines also subjugated peoples and races as the "other" to be dominated. Moreover, it defines women not just as the other of men but also as subordinated to men in power insofar as it conceives of society in analogy to the patriarchal household that was sustained by slave labor. Women of color and poor women are doubly and triply oppressed in such a patriarchal societal system. Therefore a critical feminist theology of liberation does not speak of male oppressors and female oppressed, of all men over and against all women but about patriarchy as a pyramidal system and hierarchical structure of society and church in which women's oppression is specified not only in terms of race and class but also in terms of marital status. The patriarchal victimization and dehumanization of the "poorest and most despised women on earth"[2] (Redstockings) exhibits the full death-dealing powers of patriarchy, while their struggles for liberation and their survival expresses the fullest experience of God's grace and power in our midst. Such a universal understanding of feminist liberation was already articulated by black activist Anna Cooper in 1892:

Let women's claim to be as broad in the concrete as in the abstract. We take our stand on the solidarity of humanity, the oneness of life, and the unnaturalness and injustice of all special favoritism, whether of sex, race, country, or condition. . . . The colored woman feels that women's cause is one and universal; and that not till the image of God, whether in parian or ebony, is sacred and inviolable; not till race, color, sex, and condition are seen as accidents, and not the substance of life; not till the universal title of humanity to life, liberty, and the pursuit of happiness is conceded to be inalienable to all; not till then is woman's cause won—not the white woman's, nor the black woman's, nor the red woman's, but the cause of every man and every woman who has writhed silently under a mighty wrong. Woman's wrongs are thus indissolubly linked with all undefended woe and the acquirement of her "rights" will mean the final triumph of all right over might; the supremacy of the moral forces of reason, and justice, and love in the government of the nations of earth.[3]

A feminist theology of liberation must remain first and foremost a critical theology of liberation as long as women suffer the injustice and oppression of patriarchal structures. It explores the particular experiences of women struggling for liberation from systemic patriarchy and at the same time indicts all patriarchal structures and texts, especially those of biblical religion. Such a theology seeks to name theologically the alienation, anger, pain, and dehumanization of women engendered by patriarchal sexism and racism in society and church. At the same time it seeks to articulate an alternative vision of liberation by exploring women's experiences of survival and salvation in their struggle against patriarchal oppression and degradation, as well as by assessing Christian texts, traditions, and communities in terms of such liberation from patriarchal oppression.

Such a critical feminist theology of liberation does not advocate the co-optation of women's religious powers by ecclesiastical patriarchy nor the feminist abandonment of biblical vision and community. Its feminist heuristic key is not a dual theological anthropology of masculine and feminine, nor the concept of the complementarity of the sexes, nor a metaphysical principle of female ascendancy. Its formulations are based on the radical assumption that gender is socially, politically, economically, and theologically constructed, and that such a social construction serves to perpetuate the patriarchal exploitation and oppression of all women which is most fully expressed in the fate of the "poorest and most despised women on the earth."

A feminist critical theology of liberation seeks to enable Christian women to explore theologically the structural sin of patriarchal sexism, in a feminist conversion to reject its spiritual internalizations, and to become in such a conversion the *ekklesia* of women, women-church. In exorcising the internalized structural evil of patriarchal sexism, as well as in calling the whole church to conversion and repentance, Christian feminism and feminist theology reclaim the right and power to articulate our own theology, to reclaim our own spirituality, and to determine our own and our sisters' religious life. As the church of women we celebrate our religious powers and ritualize our visions for change and liberation. We bond together in struggling with all women for liberation, and we share our strength in nurturing each other in the full awareness and and recognition that the church of women is always the *ecclesia reformanda*, the church on the way in need of conversion and "revolutionary patience" with our own failures as well as with those of our sisters. Concern for reconciliation is pivotal for such a process of becoming "a people of God." We need to listen to each other's experiences, to cease speaking for all women, and to overcome in solidarity and support our guilt reactions.

To advocate as the hermeneutical center of a feminist critical theology of liberation the women's liberation movement in biblical religion, to speak of the "church of women" does not advocate a separatist strategy but underlines the visibility of women in biblical religion and safeguards our freedom from spiritual male control. Just as we speak of the church of the poor, of an African or Asian church, or Presbyterian, Episcopalian, or Roman Catholic churches without relinquishing our theological vision of the universal catholic Christian church, so it is also justified to speak of the church of women as a manifestation of this universal church. Since all Christian churches suffer from the structural evil of patriarchal sexism and racism in various degrees, the church of women as a feminist movement of self-identified women and women-identified men transcends all traditional "man-made" denominational lines. Its commitment and mission is defined by the solidarity with the most despised women suffering from the triple oppression of sexism, racism, and poverty. A feminist biblical interpretation of the Bible that develops within the framework of a critical theology of liberation must be situated within the feminist community of women in biblical religion.

THE BIBLE AS THE BOOK OF WOMEN-CHURCH

Taking as our hermeneutical criterion the authority of women's experience struggling for liberation, we must ask whether and how the Bible as the product of a patriarchal culture and expressed in androcentric language can also be the sacred scripture for the church of women. This is a difficult question since the Bible has been used to halt the emancipation of women, slaves, and colonialized peoples. Elizabeth Cady Stanton has eloquently summed up this use of the Bible against women's demand for political and ecclesial equality:

From the inauguration of the movement for woman's emancipation the Bible has been used to hold her in the "divinely ordained sphere" prescribed in the Old and New Testaments. . . . Creeds, codes, Scriptures and statutes are all based on this idea.[4]

Whenever women protest against political discrimination, economic exploitation, sexual violence, or our secondary status in biblical religion, the Bible is invoked against such claims. At the same time the Bible has not only served to justify theologically the oppression of women, slaves, or the poor, but it also has provided authorization for Christian women and men who rejected slavery, poverty, and patriarchal sexism as against God's will.

While in the last century clergymen invoked the Bible in order to bar women from speaking in public and in this century from becoming ordained to the priesthood, women have pointed to other biblical texts and insisted on the right interpretation of the Bible in order to legitimize their claim to public speaking and the ministry. While many feminists reject the Bible as totally oppressive and patriarchal, others have attempted to show that the Bible, correctly interpreted, preaches the emancipation of women. While Christian apologists argue that only feminist ignorance or misunderstanding leads to the rejection of the Bible, Christian biblicists maintain that feminism is a perversion of God's word and godless humanism. While Christian feminists seek for a "usable past," Christian conservatives claim that women can find happiness only by living out the scriptural injunctions to submission.

In this political-religious controversy, the women-passages in scripture are used as prooftexts for justifying one's own political-ecclesial interests. Central to this apologetic debate is the interest in legitimizing one's own position with reference to biblical authority. The detractors as well as the defenders of women's liberation refer to the Bible because of its ecclesial authority and societal influence. The focal point of this political apologetics is the Bible, but not the experience of women insofar as both sides seek to prove or disprove the patriarchal character of certain biblical texts.

However, postbiblical feminists do not challenge just certain passages and statements of the Bible; they reject the Bible as a whole as irredeemable for feminists. Recognizing that androcentric language and patriarchal traditions have erased women from biblical texts and made us "nonbeings" in biblical history, they argue that the Bible is not retrievable for feminists who are committed to women's struggle for liberation. The Bible ignores women's experience, speaks of God in male language, and sustains women's powerlessness in society and church. It legitimizes women's societal and ecclesial subordination and second-class status as well as male dominance and violence against women, especially against those caught in patriarchal marriage relationships. Because of its androcentric-patriarchal character, feminists cannot but reject the authority of the Bible. Revisionist interpretations are at best a waste of time and at worst a co-optation of feminism for patriarchal biblical religion.

Christian apologists as well as postbiblical feminists not only overlook the experiences of women in biblical religion but also assume that the Bible has authority independently of the community to which it belongs. Insofar as this apologetic debate either seeks to salvage or to reject the religious authority of the Bible for women today, it understands the Bible as a mythical archetype rather than as a historical prototype open to feminist theological transformation. As mythical archetype the Bible can only be either accepted or rejected, but not critically evaluated. A mythical archetype takes historically limited experiences and texts and posits them as universals that become authoritative and normative for all times and cultures. For instance, many scriptural texts speak of God as a male, patriarchal, all-powerful ruler. Therefore, it is argued, feminists have to accept the patriarchal male language and God of the Bible, or they have to reject the Bible and leave behind biblical religion.

By giving universal ramifications to specific historical texts and cultural situations the mythical archetype establishes an ideal form for all times that represents unchanging patterns of behavior and theological structures for the community in which it functions as sacred scripture. The Bible as archaic myth therefore constitutes the enduring order and perspective of biblical religion, reflecting unchangeable ontological patterns and perennial models for human behavior and communal life. Since biblical texts as the Word of God are formulated in androcentric language and are products and reflections of patriarchal cultures, they express a patriarchal system and androcentric world view valid for all times.

Insofar as the Bible is stamped by patriarchal oppression but claims to be the Word of God, it perpetuates an archetypal oppressive myth that cannot but be rejected by feminists on the one hand and must be maintained over and against feminism by biblical religion on the other hand. However, the archetypal myth of the Bible as the Word of God has been challenged by historical-critical scholarship and has undergone significant modifications in the last centuries. Although biblical and theological scholarship is well aware of the difficulties raised by such an archetypal understanding of the Bible, ecclesiastical authority and popular preaching have not quite accepted the challenge of historical-critical scholarship to the archetypal definition of biblical inspiration.

In the dominant paradigm of biblical interpretation, three

hermeneutical models are interrelated, but can be distinguished. *First,* the doctrinal model of interpretation centers around the teachings and creeds of the church and refers to the Bible in order to prove and substantiate patriarchal teachings and symbolic structures. For instance, the debate on whether Paul teaches the subordination of women or allows for the full equality of women in the church, and therefore for women's ordination, is situated within the ambience of this doctrinal model. This model subscribes fully to the archetypal understanding of the Bible, especially if it understands it in a literalist way and conceives of biblical revelation as verbal inspiration. Although evangelical feminism modifies this doctrinal model, it seeks to remain within the boundaries set by it in order to remain faithful to biblical revelation.

The *second* model in biblical interpretation could be termed the historical-factual model. It was developed over and against the doctrinal model and often identifies biblical truth and authority with historical or textual facticity. The Bible must be understood as a collection of historical writings that are more or less true, that is, historically reliable. However, the canonical collection of early Christian writings is not comprehensive, and therefore historical critical scholarship must study all early Christian writings that are still extant today. The truth of biblical religion resides in those traditions and texts that are historically reliable, that is, tell us what actually happened. Biblical authority is understood in terms of historical facticity. If, for instance, scholars can prove that the "empty tomb stories" in the New Testament are secondary legends of the community, then they cannot accord historical reliability and theological significance to the resurrection witness of Mary Magdalene and the women disciples. Or, if Jesus chose only men and not women as his followers, then he established a pattern for all times and women cannot become apostolic successors and be ordained as priests. This model thus establishes the archetypal significance of the Bible through historical verification.

The *third* model of biblical interpretation could be termed the dialogic-pluralistic model of form and redaction criticism that seeks to recover *all* the canonical texts and traditions and to understand them as theological responses to their historical-communal situations. The Bible becomes a kaleidoscope mirroring and reflecting the pluralistic and multifaceted life and faith of biblical communities in their historical-cultural circumstances.

However, the Bible contains not only a variety of texts but also many contradictory or even oppressive texts and symbols that cannot all have the same theological authority for communities today. While this dialogic-pluralistic model moves away from the archetypal understanding of the Bible in its historical-critical interpretations, it resorts again to the archetypal paradigm in its theological evaluations and normative claims whenever it seeks to identify God's voice in the polyphony of biblical voices. Acknowledging the pluriform theological character of the canon, it must establish a "canon within the canon," a theological criterion and measuring rod with which to assess the truth and authority of the various biblical texts and traditions. This "measure" is derived from the canon, which is the collection of biblical writings acknowledged by Christians as sacred scriptures. This attempt to define a "canonical" criterion began with Marcion in the second century A.D. and has become especially important for the dialogic-pluralistic understanding of the Bible.

In response to the factual-historical model the neoorthodox "canon within the canon" debate attempts to theologically identify those texts and traditions of the Bible that can serve as measuring rods for evaluating the pluralistic collection of canonical writings as to their truth-claims. This neoorthodox model does no longer understand the whole Bible as archetypal myth but only those texts and traditions that are judged "canonical," that is, as expressing the Word of God. It identifies such a "canon" either along historical-factual lines (for example, the authentic Jesus-traditions, the *ipsissima verba* of Jesus, or the earliest traditions of the apostolic church), along doctrinal lines (the gospel message; the Pauline doctrine of justification by faith; the creed) or along philosophical lines of argument (for example, revelatory essence and historical accidental statements; timeless truth and culturally conditioned language; universal revelation and historical expression; constant tradition and changing traditions; the liberating impulses of the biblical vision and its oppressive patriarchal articulations).

Such a search for a fixed point of revelation or a normative tradition in the shifting sand of cultural-historical pluralism is also found in feminist theology. For instance, Rosemary Radford Ruether has proposed the distinction between the liberating-prophetic critique or biblical religion and its cultural deformations,[5] whereas Letty Russell has reformulated her distinction of Tradition and traditions with reference to the eschatological future of God's liberation: "The Bible has authority because it witnesses to God's liberating action on behalf of God's creation."[6] However, the attempt to derive a universal principle or normative tradition from particular historical texts and specific cultural situations indicates that such a feminist theological hermeneutics still adheres to the archetypal biblical paradigm that establishes universal principles and normative patterns. Since it is impossible for feminist theologians to accept *all* canonical texts and traditions, they must claim that certain texts or traditions are not deformed by androcentrism and patriarchy if they want to reclaim the Bible as normative and authoritative for feminists in biblical religion.

However, such a feminist hermeneutics should take into account more seriously the androcentric character of biblical language, on the one hand, and the patriarchal stamp of all biblical traditions, on the other hand. By distinguishing language and content, patriarchal expression and liberating tradition, androcentric text and feminist "witness," it relies on an untenable linguistic-philosophical position that divides form and content, linguistic expression and revelatory truth. By choosing one tradition, text, or biblical trajectory, it advocates a reductionist method of theological critique that relinquishes the historical richness of biblical experience.

A feminist critical interpretation of the Bible, I would therefore argue, cannot take as its point of departure the normative authority of the biblical archetype, but must begin with women's experience in their struggle for liberation. In doing so it subjects the Bible to a critical feminist scrutiny and to the theological authority of the church of women that seeks to assess the oppressive or liberative dynamics of all biblical texts and their function in the contemporary feminist struggle for liberation. Just as Jesus, according to the gospels, realized freedom towards scripture and tradition for the sake of human well-being and wholeness

(Mark 2:27), so also a feminist critical hermeneutics seeks to assess the function of the Bible in terms of women's liberation and wholeness. It follows Augustine, Thomas, and the Vatican Council II[7] in formulating a criterion or canon that limits inspired truth and revelation to matters pertaining to the salvation, freedom, and liberation of all, especially of women.

However, it derives such a "canon" *not* from the biblical writings but from the contemporary struggle of women against racism, sexism, and poverty as oppressive systems of patriarchy and from its systemic explorations in feminist theory. It can do so because it does not understand the Bible as perduring archetype but as historical prototype or as formative root-model of biblical faith and life. Its vision of liberation and salvation is informed by the biblical prototype but not derived from it. It places biblical texts under the authority of feminist experience insofar as it maintains that revelation is ongoing and takes place "for the sake of our salvation." It does not seek for identification with certain biblical texts and traditions, but for solidarity with women in biblical religion. As the church of women, we are not called to reproduce biblical structures and traditions, but to remember and transform our biblical heritage.

The understanding of the Bible as a historical prototype rather than as a mythical archetype allows the church of women to make connections with our own experiences, historical struggles, and feminist options in order to create visions for the future out of these interconnections between women's struggle for liberation and biblical religion. It enables us to make choices between oppressive and liberative traditions of the Bible without having to accept or reject it as a whole. In such a process of feminist critical evaluation and assessment, the Bible functions no longer as authoritative source but as a multifaceted resource for women's struggle for liberation. Insofar as the Bible is the formative root-model of Christian life and community, a feminist critical interpretation has to explore *all* dimensions of the biblical text and tradition as well as its contemporary functions in order to assess their structural impact and religious-cultural influence on women today, whether they are members of the church of women or not. Such a feminist paradigm of critical interpretation is not based on a faithful adherence to biblical texts or obedient submission to biblical authority, but on the solidarity with the women of the past and of the present whose lives and struggles are touched by the biblical trajectory in Western culture.

TOWARD A FEMINIST MODEL OF BIBLICAL INTERPRETATION

To make the systematically articulated feminist experience of the church of women central to biblical interpretation and theological reflection requires a paradigm shift in biblical interpretation, a shift from the understanding of the Bible as archetypal myth to its understanding as a historical prototype. In the context of such a paradigm shift, a feminist model of critical interpretation is emerging that is committed to the church of women and women's struggle for liberation. As far as I can see, this interpretive model of a critical feminist theology of liberation is in the process of developing four structural elements constitutive for a feminist biblical interpretation.

Since all biblical texts are formulated in androcentric language and reflect patriarchal societal structures, a feminist critical interpretation begins with a *hermeneutics of suspicion* rather than with a hermeneutics of consent and affirmation. It develops a *hermeneutics of proclamation* rather than a hermeneutics of historical factuality because the Bible still functions as holy scripture in Christian communities today. Rather than reduce the liberating impulse of the Bible to a feminist principle or one feminist biblical tradition, it develops a *hermeneutics of remembrance* that moves from biblical texts about women to the reconstruction of women's history. Finally, a feminist model of critical interpretation moves from a hermeneutics of disinterested distance to a *hermeneutics of creative actualization* that involves the church of women in the imaginative articulation of women's biblical story and its ongoing history and community.

First: A *hermeneutics of suspicion* does not presuppose the feminist authority and truth of the Bible but takes as its starting point the assumption that biblical texts and their interpretations are androcentric and serve patriarchal functions. Since most of the biblical writings are ascribed to male authors and most of the biblical interpreters in church and academy are men, such an assumption is justified. Just as the woman in the parable sweeps the whole house in search of her lost coin, so feminist critical interpretation searches for the lost traditions and visions of liberation among its inheritance of androcentric-biblical texts and their interpretations. In order to unearth a "feminist coin" from the biblical tradition, it critically analyzes contemporary scholarly and popular interpretations, the tendencies of the biblical writers and traditioning processes themselves, and the theoretical models underlying contemporary biblical-historical and theological interpretations.

In the past years feminist scholarship has cleared away many androcentric mistranslations, patriarchal interpretations, and one-sided reconstructions of biblical scholars. Among the "coins" found are the maternal God-language of the Old Testament, which especially Phyllis Trible has rediscovered, women's apostleship and leadership in the early Christian movement which I have underlined, and the leadership of women in the ancient synagogue, which Bernadette Brooten has retrieved from male scholarly prejudice.[8] Feminist critical scholarship has also pointed to the androcentric tendencies and patriarchal interests of biblical writers and of the canonization process in the so-called patristic period. Such tendencies can be traced in, for example, the different Old Testament references to the prophet Myriam, or in the way Luke plays down the apostleship of women and the writer of the Pastorals reintroduces a patriarchal model of biblical community, or in the canonical exclusion of traditions of so-called heretical movements.

A feminist hermeneutics of suspicion also questions the underlying presuppositions, androcentric models, and unarticulated interests of contemporary biblical interpretation. Feminist scholarship has questioned the unreflected androcentric world view and patriarchal interpretive models presupposed by biblical scholarship. The very fact that we study only the statements of biblical writers about women, but not about men, reflects an androcentric theoretical-cultural paradigm which understands man as the paradigmatic human being and woman as the "other," the exception but not the rule. Biblical scholarship thus reproduces the effects of androcentric biblical language that generally subsumes woman under the generic "man" and "he." Because scholars do not recognize the dynamics of this interpretive model of androcentrism, they do not understand that all androcentric language must be understood as generic language until proven otherwise. All androcentric biblical texts must therefore be assumed to speak about men and women unless women and female aspects are explicitly excluded.

Such a hermeneutics of suspicion has therefore far-reaching consequences for the question of biblical translation, which has received much intention in recent years. The mass media have dubbed the search for an inclusive translation of the Bible as the "castration" of the Bible, whereas the political right sees it as one of the gravest aberrations of the National Council of Churches. The emotional reactions to the proposal of inclusive translation indicate the political importance of this issue. Since language shapes our self-understanding and world view, the problem of inclusive biblical translation is not a trivial issue. If it is true that "the limits of our language are the limits of our world," then androcentric biblical language and its translation becomes a feminist issue of utmost importance. Such language not only marginalizes women but also makes us invisible in the written classics of our culture, among which the Bible is preeminent.

An adequate biblical translation must render androcentric language differently at a time when androcentric language no longer is understood as generic language. Faithfulness to the biblical texts means to translate those texts which are patriarchal with grammatically masculine language, and those texts which are not with grammatically feminine and masculine terms with generic human words. Therefore such a critical translation requires a feminist critical assessment and evaluation of the patriarchal oppressive or generic liberative dynamics of individual texts. A historically adequate translation must not either further patriarchalize biblical generic texts, on the one hand, or veil their patriarchal character and impact in generic language, on the other hand. Feminist linguists have given us some guidelines for recognizing when language functions in a sexist way: Sexist language creates the linguistic invisibility or marginality of women; it describes women as dependent and as derived from men; it characterizes women in stereotypical roles and images; it ridicules women and trivilializes their contributions; it mentions women only when they are the exceptions or present a problem; and it singles them out from the collective, for example, blacks, Jews, Third World peoples, as if women did not belong to each of these groups. A hermeneutics of suspicion must test not just the original biblical texts but also contemporary translations as to how much they succumb to linguistic sexism.

Second: While a historically adequate translation of the Bible has to bring to the fore the sexist-patriarchal as well as the feminist inclusive character of biblical texts, a *hermeneutics of proclamation* has to assess its theological significance and power for the contemporary community of faith. Faithfulness to the struggle of women for liberation requires an evaluative theological judgment and insistence that oppressive patriarchal texts and sexist traditions cannot claim the authority of divine revelation. Such oppressive texts and traditions must be denounced as androcentric articulations of patriarchal interests and structures. Such texts must be tested not only with respect to their sexism but also with respect to their racism and colonial militarism. Such a historical-critical assessment must be complemented by a political-critical feminist evaluation which seeks to assess the interaction of patriarchal biblical texts with contemporary culture. Rather than to free women from cultural stereotypes and oppression, patriarchal texts reinforce cultural stereotypes and patriarchal submission. They do so, not because they are misinterpreted, but because they are formulated in order to legitimate patriarchal oppression.

Yet not only historical patriarchal texts but also from a historical point of view, feminist-neutral or even feminist-positive texts of the Bible can function to reinforce patriarchal structures if they are proclaimed or taught in order to assure patriarchal behavior and inculcate oppressive values. If, for example, a battered woman is told to take up her cross and to suffer as Jesus did in order to save her marriage, then such feminist-neutral biblical motives are used for reinforcing patriarchal submission. Similarly, in our culture that socializes primarily women into altruism and selfless love, the biblical commandment of love and call for service can be culturally misused to sustain women's patriarchal exploitation. A feminist hermeneutics of proclamation must therefore critically analyze the intersection of biblical texts with contemporary patriarchal culture and values.

In conclusion, a feminist hermeneutics of proclamation has, on the one hand, to insist that all texts that are identified as sexist or patriarchal should not be retained in the lectionary and be proclaimed in Christian worship or catechesis. On the other hand, those texts that in a feminist critical process of evaluation are identified as transcending their patriarchal contexts and as articulating a liberating vision of human freedom and wholeness should receive their proper place in the liturgy and teaching of the churches. In short, a feminist critical translation of the Bible must be complemented by a careful theological evaluation of biblical texts and their oppressive or liberative impact in specific cultural situations.

Third: Such a feminist hermeneutics of proclamation must be balanced by a critical *hermeneutics of remembrance* that recovers *all* biblical traditions through a historical-critical reconstruction of biblical history from a feminist perspective. Rather than relinquishing androcentric biblical texts and patriarchal traditions, a hermeneutics of remembrance seeks to utilize historical-critical analysis in order to move beyond the androcentric text to the history of women in biblical religion.[9] If feminist identity is not based on the experience of biological sex or on essential gender differences, but on the common historical experience of women as collaborating or struggling participants in patriarchal culture and biblical history, then the reconstruction of early Christian history in a feminist perspective is not just a historical-critical but also a feminist-theological task. Feminist meaning cannot only be derived from the egalitarian surplus of androcentric texts, but must also be found in and through androcentric texts and patriarchal history.

Rather than abandon the memory of our foresisters' sufferings and hopes in our patriarchal Christian past, a hermeneutics of remembrance *reclaims* their sufferings and struggles in and through the subversive power of the "remembered past." If the enslavement and colonialization of peoples becomes total when their history is destroyed and the solidarity with the dead is made impossible, then a feminist biblical hermeneutics of remembrance has the task of becoming a "dangerous memory"[10] that reclaims the visions and sufferings of the dead. Such a "subversive memory" not only keeps alive the sufferings and hopes of women in the biblical past, but also allows for a universal solidarity of sisterhood among women of the past, present, and future. The continuing challenge of the victims of religious patriarchy is not met by the denial of their self-understanding and religious vision as mistaken or as ideological self-deception, but only in and through engaged solidarity and committed remembrance of their hopes and despairs in the church of women.

Such a feminist hermeneutics of remembrance proposes theoretical models for historical reconstructions that place women not on the periphery but in the center of biblical community and theology. Insofar as androcentric biblical texts not only reflect their patriarchal-cultural environment but also allow a glimpse of the early Christian movements as the discipleship of equals, the reality of women's commitment and leadership in these movements precedes the patriarchal injunctions of the New Testament. Although the canon preserves only remnants of such a nonpatriarchal Christian ethos, these remnants still allow us to recognize that such a patriarchalization process is not inherent in Christian community but progressed only slowly and with difficulty. Therefore, a feminist hermeneutics of remembrance can reclaim early Christian theology and history as our own theology and history. Women as church have a continuous history and tradition that can claim the discipleship of equals as its biblical roots.

In short, a feminist hermeneutics of remembrance has as its primary task to keep alive the *memoria passionis* of biblical women, as well as to reclaim our biblical heritage. However, this heritage is misrepresented when it is understood solely as a history of patriarchal oppression. It also must be reconstituted as a history of liberation and religious agency. The history and theology of women's oppression perpetuated by patriarchal biblical texts and clerical patriarchy must be understood for what it is. This history and theology must not be allowed to cancel out the memory of the struggle, life, and leadership of biblical women who spoke and acted in the power of the Spirit.

Fourth: Such historical reconstructions of women's biblical history need to be supplemented by a *hermeneutics of creative actualization* that expresses the active engagement of women in the ongoing biblical story of liberation. While a feminist hermeneutics of remembrance is interested in historical-critical reconstruction, a feminist hermeneutics of creative actualization allows women to enter the biblical story with the help of historical imagination, artistic recreation, and liturgical ritualization. A feminist biblical interpretation, therefore, must not only be critical but also constructive, not only be oriented toward the past but also toward the future of women-church.

Such a hermeneutics of creative actualization seeks to retell biblical stories from a feminist perspective, to reformulate biblical visions and injunctions in the perspective of the discipleship of equals, and to create midrashic amplifications of the feminist remnants that have survived in patriarchal texts. In this process of creative re-vision it utilizes all available means of artistic imagination, literary creativity, music, and dance. The Bible as formative prototype has inspired artistic creativity and legendary embellishments throughout the centuries. In midrash and apocryphal writings, in liturgy and sacred hymns, the patriarchal church has ritualized certain aspects of the biblical story and celebrated the "founding fathers" of biblical religion.

A feminist hermeneutics of creative actualization reclaims for the church of women the same imaginative freedom, popular creativity, and ritual powers. Women today not only rewrite biblical stories about women, but also reformulate patriarchal prayers and create feminist rituals celebrating our ancestors. We rediscover in story and poetry, in drama and liturgy, in song and dance, our biblical foresisters' sufferings and victories. In feminist liturgy and haggada, women retell the story of the Passover or that of the "last supper." We re-vision the liturgy of Advent or the baptismal ritual. In ever new images and symbols we seek to rename the God of the Bible and the significance of Jesus. We not only spin tales about the voyages of Prisca, the missionary, or about Junia, the apostle, but also dance Sarah's circle and experience prophetic enthusiasm. We sing litanies of praise to our foresisters and pray laments of mourning for the lost stories of our foremothers. Only by reclaiming our religious imagination and our sacred powers of naming can women-church "dream new dreams and see new visions."

We do so, however, in the full awareness that such creative participation in the biblical story must be won in and through a feminist critical process of interpretation that repents of the structural sin and internalized values of patriarchal sexism. The religious creativity and feminist power of re-creation actualized in the church of women seem to me the feminist "leaven" of the bakerwoman God that will transform patriarchal biblical religion so that the biblical story will become truly a resource for all who seek for a sustaining vision in their struggle for liberation from patriarchal oppression.

3. The Feminist Redemption of Christ

RITA NAKASHIMA BROCK

Every summer since 1977 I have spent a week in August with 180 high school students and twenty-five adults in a process that is a magical 160 hours. Most of us strangers to each other, we are thrown together in a program designed to confront social issues such as racial and sexual identity, sexism, racism, and family interactions. The "Brother/Sisterhood Camp" is a project of the National Conference of Christians and Jews. Those precious days buoy my spirits all year and haunt me when I capitulate to flabby, dishonest relationships.

The annual magic is conjured when we connect beyond the level of our most competent, "together" identities, and the realness of the pain we all carry inside us becomes a healing power. A deeper connecting begins to allow change to happen and healing energies to surface. One moment in the week that the connecting happens always astounds me with its power.

An invited speaker talks to everyone about the fear and anger women feel at the threat of rape and about the real damage done long after the deed has happened. The speaker is angry, and she speaks with the force of her anger and of her concern for women. Some males react with hostility or defensiveness. Suddenly, the speaker stops and asks the women in the room to share their anger, their feelings about rape. The rape survivors,

Rita Nakashima Brock is on the faculty of the department of theology at Valparaiso University, Valparaiso, Ind. She has also taught at Chapman College, Scripps College, and Jarvis Christian College. A Ph.D. candidate at the Claremont Graduate School, Ms. Brock is working on a dissertation on feminism and Christology. She also writes on Asian women's theology and feminist understandings of freedom.

with support from their sisters, tell the horrifying tales and bare the hidden scars. Permission has been given for the truth to be told. The males are abruptly confronted, not by some strange speaker—one of those "libbers"—but by the female campers they have come to know and care about. Slowly, in the excruciating sharing of pain and terror, a transformation happens. A severer listening, a deeper hearing is taking place.

Two events begin in those moments of truth spoken. The dominant-male/submissive-female ritual is exposed by those with the courage to name the truth of their lives. Behind the male hostility and defensiveness are fear, profound loneliness, and a raging sense of inadequacy—feelings embraced openly by many for the first time. With the embracing comes new feelings of shared pain with the women who speak. No longer just a victim's pain, the pain has become the shared hurt of honest relationships in which brokenness is fiercely named. And for those who had the courage to hear, to feel, and to speak, a new empowerment begins. As one woman decides to say her life is important to her, and in her fear she tells the truth of her existence, others rise to support her and claim themselves. For some, the glimpses of transformation and empowerment illumine enough to light a way dimly to wholeness; for others they become a long-forgotten dream.

The images of transformation and empowerment in those annual events seep through the issues in this chapter like a permanent stain. Those brief, healing, summer hours lurk behind my every religious question, including the one presented here—the question of feminism and Christology.

Essential to that ancient dominant-submissive rape ritual are the rules that give no power and authority to women except through our connections to male institutions and our relationships of submission to men. In Christianity, are women therefore redeemed and legitimated by our reconciliation to the saving efficacy of a male savior? Even if we reconceive deity as goddess, what do we do with Jesus Christ? If we have felt the power of that symbol called Jesus Christ, what choices do we have?

THE UNHOLY GOODNESS OF
PATRIARCHAL DUALISM

Connecting feminist images of whole, healed life in a pluralistic world—images of transformation and empowerment—with what has been presented in most traditional Christologies appears impossible. The theologians of the tradition have given us a dualistic, hierarchal Christ, a Christ who divides the world into true believers and heretics. Christ is the absolute word of God, the center of faith, and the basis for all action. This Christ is lord over all and servant to all, perfect in any form, a judgment on humanity as sinful, and a sign of everyone's need to be saved from what is most frightening.

Christology takes a first-century Jewish male and makes authoritative, exclusive claims about his divinity, using writings that are already imaginative theology. This chapter is a study of the damaging effects of those claims on women and a presentation of feminist visions of salvation that affirm Jesus and redeem a Christ for women.

The continued insistence upon Jesus' human perfection as evidence of a divine presence in him removes him from the human sphere. If he is the perfect manifestation of divine love, or human faith, or whatever else is claimed, the assumptions are already made that only one perfect form can exist and that we have the right to proclaim that one form as supremely immanent divine grace. However, a relational view of reality understands all "ideal" forms as related to context. We must ask who determines what is ideal and how the determination is made. Of the life of Jesus we are only allowed shadowy glimpses, veiled in New Testament theological claims full of early church social-political agendas, agendas including the patriarchal demand to make absolute either/or choices on the basis of the "ideal" divine incarnation.

One way patriarchy limits the possible fullness of our world is to reduce all questions to either/or. The presupposition that a past and fixed understanding of any tradition dictates all that it has actually been, or what it can become, is false. The relation between feminism and Christianity is far more fluid and promising if we refuse a future determined by a patriarchally defined past. All images are created out of a past but are not determined by any one interpretation of that past. The demand to draw battle lines across the fields of reified, exclusivistic images and to pick the "right" side is the demand that brings our age to the brink of nuclear annihilation. When we think in the terms of war, we give credence to the presuppositions that make war. We must think beyond the divided patriarchal mind and the wars it creates.

Beneath the demand to choose divided sides is the ideology of dualism, an ideology that abstracts good and evil from their presence in living contexts. As long as we think in an ideal and abstract world, out of the traffic of deeply lived experience, a dualism is conceivable, but it cannot be experienced. As soon as we enter the ambiguous arena of concrete reality, the insistence that sides be absolute does violence to actual persons. Dualism rejects evil without understanding its root causes and, therefore, does not heal or transform evil. Instead, dualism hides from evil in fixed forms and divided sides.

The notions of goodness and perfection that emerge from dualism are static and brittle. This is unholy goodness; it does not arise from reality in process-as-lived, nor from the ability to hold distinctions without collapsing them into absolute, fixed dualisms. Unholy goodness demands allegiance by insisting on its own reality as unalterably absolute and by rejecting anything that questions it. The dualism behind static understandings of goodness is nonrelational and destructive of persons.

Pornography and Silence: Culture's Revenge Against Nature by Susan Griffin is a stunning and compassionate look at patriarchal dualism's destruction of life. What Griffin calls the pornographic mind is the dualistic thinking that enshrouds us all. To be a product of this culture and its images is to be affected by this mind and all its variations. The pornographic mind lurks in the interstices of conscious thoughts, in catacombs of fear, deeply buried and ready to explode its destructive forces in moments of fear and crisis.[1]

The pornographic mind is fed by fear of itself as a part of vulnerable creatures. Hence, it traffics in absolutes. The mind represses what it fears by denying its own inner yearnings and projects what it fears upon others. The pornographic mind then destroys the "other" whom it fears because the "other" reminds it of its own vulnerability. This mind is bent upon self-destruction, lying to itself about what it destroys in its objectified images. In the scurrying to hide in its own illusory images, the mind affects history and culture in profound ways by insisting its images determine all reality.

The pornographic mind uses its images to kill what grounds us in relationships. This mind fears feeling, feeling that arises from our connection to self, to nature, and to others. Thus the pornographic mind creates cultural demons in which to hide and dehumanized, objectified images to abuse. It creates the lie that relationships are not what ground us in ourselves, others, and life itself.

When a pornographic culture attempts to replace its own demons for the myths and symbols that help us find our way back to a whole reality, the basic yearning that leads us to others and self-discovery is destroyed, crushed, lost. Griffin calls this yearning *eros*. But the pornographic mind fears intimate relationship, with self or other. Eros, however, will not be forgotten; its power becomes thwarted and leads to self-destruction.[2] For eros to be reborn in us, all that patriarchal culture has named evil must be reclaimed as part of ourselves—sensuality, change, darkness, self-affirmation, nature, death, passion, woman.

The mind divided against itself must reconnect the dualisms that divide it and rediscover the yearning toward union—toward eros—a union dangerous to patriarchal culture. This dangerous need for relationship must become part of our religious symbol system so that nature and culture may be reunited. For religion to become a healing force in our lives again, the life-denying, otherworldliness of faith must reunite nature and culture so we can become whole again. With the reuniting, we become creators—vulnerable, feeling, dancing—and parts of an ineffable ecstasy that binds us to the deepest whirling mystery within ourselves, to the unspeakable mystery of the sacred.

As our yearning for ourselves and others leads us, we continue to confront, however, the impassable dualism of good and evil and its absolute forms of unchanging goodness and perfection. We lose ourselves in our search for truth. We accept the system and insist on cleanly divided camps of good and evil.

THE HOLY GOODNESS OF PRESENCE

Christological claims about the person of Jesus are grist for the dualistic mill that devours us. Jesus is claimed to be perfect as a man (*sic*). His perfection is what shows the divine presence, already understood as static perfection, to be incarnate in him. Then, the ideal activity of this perfect "god-man" was to be the victim of destructive, evil forces that kill him. Ultimately, however, the forces are defeated because an omnipotent deity delivers him into an abstract, nonpresent existence. To be worthy of God's saving grace, we must reach God through the perfection of Jesus. To be protected from evil we must become passive victims, therefore—for we cannot be perfect men.

Such Christological claims about Jesus must be purged. The implications of the claims are damaging to the feminist search for justice. To be worthy of God's protective grace and to deserve justice we are forced to strive to be self-sacrificing, passive victims. But to seek a fixed state is to stop being open to others, to cease changing and growing. If one aspect of death is the end of living relationships, the consequence of being a perfect victim is to strive to end relationships, to find death before the forces of destruction inflict it. In a living death we become worthy victims of evil. Only victims are selfless, a status many women have attempted to achieve for years.[3]

While it may at first appear to the advantage of the oppressed to be made selfless and good—the Christ-like "least of these"— the damage to the oppressed of a rigid, self-righteous dualism is devastating. The oppressed are not allowed to be angry about oppression because such "irrational, wrong" feelings indicate a lack of selflessness and goodness. The oppressed get locked into unholy goodness, playing the role of innocent victims because, when the oppressed are perceived as not being good, or worthy of justice, the underlying legitimization for justice crumbles. So when women cease being selfless and good, we do not deserve equality because we become threatening and dangerous. Angry women who refuse passivity and selflessness reject the victim status and shatter the dualism implied in that status. An equality not based on dualism insists that those with the power to grant justice are themselves not totally good or right. Thus they have no right to withhold justice.

A further disadvantage of the innocent victim status is that it immobilizes the oppressed who are unable to work through internalized forms of oppression because the approval associated with being the innocent victim is the main route to justice. We feel afraid to confront our own felt lack of goodness, our own sense of inadequacy.

When the dominant values, ideas, and attitudes of a society are not our own, but are the measuring rod for our humanity and our right to justice, we become self-haters and haters of others, for the eternal world refuses to confirm our existence. The oppressed learn to adopt the very system that is used to oppress us. Members of the dominant group create ideologies and institutions they use against all who threaten their system. The ideologies and institutions are used to subjugate and devalue the oppressed who begin to believe the system is true. When we feel wrong within a prescribed system that proscribes us, we are ashamed of ourselves. Our self-esteem is tied to self-hate as fear and shame force us to seek obsessively to be good so we will deserve justice and love. We are unable to confront not only imposed systems but even the existing, complex, negative parts of ourselves we fear. We fail to see that our self-hate leads us to devalue others. Hence, feminism has failed at many points to confront its own racism, anti-Semitism, classism, and Western imperialism. We identify ourselves solely as victim. Then, rather than seeing the damage our fear does to ourselves and others, we place all responsibility elsewhere on a one-dimensional "enemy."

The above argument does not mean that women are accomplices to or are responsible for the development of patriarchy. Women are magnificent survivors of a system designed to control, exploit, and in its most extreme forms, destroy us. Survival is no longer enough, however, for patriarchy must be shattered if our planet is to survive. Women must be empowered to love and claim ourselves in a fully open, honest way and to demand justice. And, as we are all relational beings, we must learn to face and understand the patriarchy within us that disempowers us.

But if oppressors cannot be "bad" and victims "good" (a variation of the "God is on our side" theme), then how can women defeat the misogyny that threatens us? When we deny the power of dualism and its unholy goodness, we face the question of the name in which we purge oppression. If we cannot point to the victim of oppression as "good," then how do we exorcise the demons of patriarchy? How can we demand a change from the status quo?

The demand for authoritative grounds implies that we must have an unmoving place to stand, an absolute principle we use to act for justice. Bernard Meland, in *Fallible Forms and Symbols*, calls the need for an absolute authority the "lure of certainty," a lure that supplants the authority of church and scripture with a rational certainty in an abstract absolute.

The Copernican, Freudian, and Einsteinian revolutions have challenged many of the absolute religious dogmas, power structures, and hierarchies of organized Western religions. The divine sanction given to whole categories of oppression has given way. The certainty of the Bible, divine revelation, and, finally, even abstract, absolute truth hve succumbed to the tidal wave of modern thought. Meland insists the tidal wave drowning the abstract absolute contains the most sensitive minds of our age. These minds aim at restoring our sense of reality, "at recovering it after centuries of captivity in a wasteland of conceptual abstractions."[4] Feminism is a major part of the tidal wave. We have received inheritances from minds that have made relative absolute certainty. If we now begin to insist on an absolute ground on which to gain justice, we defeat our best insights.

The demand for centralized authority, for one abstract principle that unites our cause, is the demand of totalitarianism. The demand puts us a step removed from the ambiguities of lived experience. We come to think we already know what is wrong and what is needed before we listen. In Christology the use of the cosmic Christ has functoned to muffle the cry of the human person in our presence. We are convinced we hear, instead of the person before us, the voice of Christ, and that conviction becomes a shield against our deepest hearing. Alice Walker, in her novel *The Color Purple*, poignantly describes this not-hearing when Nettie, a black woman missionary to West Africa, realizes:

The Africans never asked us to come. . . . There's no use blaming them if we feel unwelcome. . . . We try every way we can to show that love. But they reject us. . . . And if they listen they say, . . . Why don't you speak our language? . . . Why can't you remember the old ways? . . . After all . . . we can leave, they must stay. . . . God is different to us now, after all these years in Africa. More spirit than ever before, and more internal. Most people think he has to look like something or someone— . . . Christ—but we don't. And not being tied to what God looks like, frees us.[5]

To be freed of an absolute is to be freed to respond to reality from the depths of experienced reality. In that response we feel the terrible pain of things gone wrong. We recognize what is wrong because, by our authority to claim our own pain, we come to touch another's pain and it becomes ours. Fully present, we come to an awareness of what destroys life by willful destruction and of what nurtures life by the empowerment of ourselves and each other. By our lives we name what is wrong.

The actual experience and observable impact of oppression is where we begin. Victims are not to be liberated from oppression because the oppressed are good. Women will shatter patriarchy because misogyny in all its aspects—rape, the denial of power over our bodies, institutionalized poverty, and systematic limitation of access to the decision-making structures of society— harm us. The foundational strength of feminism is not a self-righteous and self-sacrificing allegiance to a central image or a totalitarian ideology, but a clear statement of experienced oppression.

We know the devastation of patriarchy. We know because it hurts us. We hurt because we also know another reality when we catch glimpses of a world beyond patriarchy. But the vision that lures us is not an absolute. Our vision emerges from an understanding of oppression and illumines a new hope drawing on resources that affirm women's reality, resources that show us the transforming presence we bring to all areas of life. An understanding of female ways of seeing and becoming and of the healing vision feminism offers comes from our experience of sisterhood, from the presence of women who hear and understand us, and from the struggle and hope we all affirm. But the new feminist vision of existence requires radical acts of rethinking and does not rely on an absolute dogmatic certainty.

The vision illuminating our demand for justice glimmers in the ambiguities of our collective experiences. The vision is energized by our persistent need to be open to ourselves and others.

Meland asserts that an attunement to and trust in the concrete exigencies of our lives and the lives of others are what reveal to us "the travail of existence . . . the cry of the human spirit . . . the pain and anguish, joy or ecstasy of fallible (humanity)."[6] Our openness and sensitivity to the complexity of existence make us hungry for a healing, restoring wholeness. If we are centered in any authority, it is not in a past person called Jesus Christ made present to us through the images created by Christology. Our authority comes from ourselves and caring relationships with those we love who suffer. This relational ability is our authority because it does not make them invisible behind an absolute. Our authority calls those we love to cease hiding behind authorities based on fear, guilt, and control. Through our authority we call them to be fully present and affirm the availability to all of the same authority.

THE HOLY GOODNESS OF EROTIC POWER

By this personal authority we rethink existence and give birth to a vision of salvation we glimpse through living experiences. Recurring within our vision of salvation is the quest for freedom. The freedom feminists seek is not, however, a state of independent self-sufficiency and is not an autonomous subject imposing its decisions against an external, passive, objectified world.[7] Feminist freedom is the ability to increase and exercise erotic power.

Erotic power is the creating, enlarging, and sustaining of relationships.[8] Erotic power is facilitating, empowering, and loving. Erotic power, as Audre Lorde explains in *Use of the Erotic: the Erotic as Power*, is the power that at its deepest roots understands joy and refuses injustice because the deepest celebration is union with others and the clearest protest against oppression comes not from an abstract commitment to principles, but from the experience of suffering caused by oppression.[9] Erotic power is to feel ourselves and others to the depths of our being, bringing us to and sustaining relationships. The truly powerful are not the hollow and afraid who control others; the truly powerful are those present to themselves and others, unafraid of change, vulnerable and open, and empowering to others.

Only when we actually engage in the difficult and painful process of deep, intimate relationships with those who threaten and frighten our securely defined selves are our whole beings pulled into new ways of understanding that heal and nurture life. The use of erotic power transcends ideology in a closed universe and reaches for understanding. Living in relational process is the erotic power that transforms, empowers, and saves our lives.

To develop and use erotic power is feminist freedom, a participation and presence in reality to the fullest extent possible. Freedom is to love ourselves and others deeply, and to be created continually by the many complex dimensions of relationship to ourselves and others. When we insist on the increase of this freedom we are led toward salvation.

Salvation is the healing of life that emerges from our freedom and from the creative imagining of a restored and whole existence. In the best of feminist visionaries such as Doris Lessing, Susan Griffin, Adrienne Rich, and Alice Walker, we encounter a persistent eros for wholeness-in-process, for self-affirmation, for relationship, for forgiveness, and for the embracing of ambiguity as a key to self-discovery.

Adrienne Rich's poetry presents a vision of salvation in vivid, passionate images of yearning and pain and of courage and hope. Rich is driven by the "passion to make and make again where such unmaking reigns."[10] Rich invisions a fluid, whole-making process and connects knowing with female embodiment. Her vision has nothing to do with greatness, exceptionalness, or eternity. Rich speaks of "care for the many-lived, unending forms in which she finds herself" until

> My heart is moved by all I cannot save:
> so much has been destroyed
> I have to cast my lot with those
> who age after age, perversely,
> with no extraordinary power,
> reconstitute the world.[11]

Alice Walker's vision of wholeness in *The Color Purple* carries an unflinching sense of tragedy while it is rich with female bonding and powerful with quiet courage, love, and healing forgiveness. The life of the main character, Celie—poor, black, ugly, and female—begins in broken despair. She believes her beloved sister Nettie is dead. She is so ashamed of her own life that she can only write letters to a God she pictures as white and male, who is the only existence left in the universe Celie believes might care about her. Celie claims back her broken life and affirms her own existence as other women love her and include Celie in their circles of relationships. When Celie discovers Nettie is alive, she stops writing to God and writes to Nettie:

> The God I been praying and writing to is a man. And act just like all the other mens I know. Trifling, forgitful and lowdown. . . . If he ever listened to poor colored women the world would be a different place, I can tell you.[12]

Through living relationships, through women who love her, Celie struggles to learn.

> God is inside you and inside everybody else. You come into the world with God. But only them that search for it inside find it. . . . God is everything. . . . Everything that is or ever was or ever will be. And when you can feel that, and be happy to feel that, you've found it . . . that feeling of being part of everything, not separate at all. . . . Everything want to be loved.[13]

This loving vision sweeps across Celie's life until its forgiveness restores even her relationship with her abusive husband, who becomes her friend. Walker paints a vision of healed life that is compelling, concrete, and visceral. The wholeness of her vision is the salvific power of real relationships, of people who hold to love despite brokenness and despair.

Lessing, Griffin, Rich, and Walker create images of salvation fraught with the contradictions of visions-as-lived, for the visions are not abstract, perfect, removed.

REDEMPTION AS HEALING

The visions are as concrete as real existence and as hopeful as the vast edges of human imagination. The visions shatter unholy goodness with breathtaking ferocity and push us to embrace and heal all of reality.

The feminist shattering of unholy goodness with a vision of healing wholeness has deep roots. Healing is one of the primary tasks of the witches.[14] Wisdom as living presence brings healing through those ancient women whose power was deeply relational and whole-making. Healing is the dominant image of much of feminism today.

Healing rejects unholy goodness. Those most wounded by reality are the most attuned to the brokenness of reality and the demands of relationships. Such sensitivity can heal. Pain is sometimes the only way to heal. When disease is deep, sometimes only a deep cut will lance the hidden infection. The healer's knife must have the courage to go deep, to the heart of the problem. Feminist anger is a deep cut. We dare not surrender our rage to safety or complacency as long as women continue to suffer the wounds of patriarchal violence. Our anger is fueled by our longings for ourselves, each other, and a reality that does not destroy us. In the images that opened this chapter, women's anger and the public naming of deep pain break open ways to transform and empower. Shared pain brings empathy and compassion.

Healing rejects coercive power and authority. Healing is its own authority. It does not come from hierarchical structures or doctoral degrees. To heal is to participate in life openly and honestly. Healing energy cannot be controlled. Because healing is not based in control, it cannot work unilaterally. The internal wisdom of each of us must participate in and want wholeness before it will come. Hence, the healer cannot dictate healing, only offer and receive it.[15]

The primary context for healing is relationships. Healing requires an empathetic, compassionate participation in the life of another. Doris Lessing, in her *Canopus in Argos* space fiction series of novels, names the quality necessary to healing the "substance-of-we-feeling," and ability to care that focuses energy and wisdom and guides them into the labyrinths of disease.[16] Healing is engaged and active. It is a gentleness that is not afraid of pain but soothes encrusted wounds and makes them whole again. Profund healing functions only when erotic power flows between persons. Each must be willing to be vulnerable and share intimate feelings. Healing requires calling up the depths of cold pain in ourselves and each other until the warmth of our own tenderness and yearning for each other makes us alive again. We destroy each other in increments by abandoning each other in our fear of what pain and the truth of our lives will do.

To discover what does not destroy us, however, more than anger and passion are required. Healing needs imagination. Not only must we strive to see those we love fully and participate in their suffering; we need also to sustain a vision of wholeness that imagines what is not yet a full reality. Imagination is a wellspring for trust and hope. Imagination must be alive in us as the searchlight for treasures yet unclaimed. Adrienne Rich's passion to "make and make again" is fed by its hungers for reclaiming what has been destroyed and what has yet to be born through acts of love.

THE REDEMPTION OF CHRIST

If Christology is to be reclaimed in feminist visions, the image of an exclusive divine presence in a "perfect" man called Jesus who came to be called the Christ is disallowed. The doctrine that only a perfect male form can incarnate God fully and be salvific makes our individual lives in female bodies a prison against God and denies our actual, sensual, changing selves as the locus of divine activity.

Christ emerges from the apostolic writings as a theological symbol system recreated by a church that uses a life-giving mythos to justify its existence.[17] Christ is a community confession created from complex relational realities. Church theologians reached back to the ancient creation myths to place the Logos at the beginning of the cosmos. It is important to see the difference between the life of these often misogynist[18] ancient symbols and the historical Jesus who is connected to the symbols, a Jesus we are only allowed to glimpse uncertainly behind the theological veils of the New Testament.

Jesus Christ need not be the authoritative center of a feminist Christian faith.[19] The demand for any unmoving center is problematic and ignores the ways in which Christological doctrines have shifted and changed with the demands of time and context. The idolatry of Jesus Christ must cease to hold us and oppress all who do not pledge allegiance to the heart of that idolatry. The demand that we give allegiance to one paradigmatic and central symbol does not do justice to our life's experiences. We live in a pluralistic universe full of complex realities that call us.

The feminist Christian commitment is not to a savior who redeems us by bringing God to us. Our commitment is to love ourselves and others into wholeness. Our commitment is to a divine presence with us here and now, a presence that works through the mystery of our deepest selves and our relationships, constantly healing us and nudging us toward a wholeness of existence we only fitfully know. That healed wholeness is not Christ; it is ourselves.

Removing the exclusive, perfect god-man Jesus Christ from the center of our Christian commitment allows us to claim ourselves and, then, to reclaim the historical Jesus and Jesus Christ. We may reclaim Jesus as a remarkable man for his time. De-divinizing him allows us to appreciate his remarkability without his humanity or theology being the measuring rod for our existence. The richness we bring to any relationship is not a humanity reduced to universal principles. Our active gift to relationships is our unique presence and the creative way we respond to, live in, and embody that context. We appreciate what we know of Jesus' particular life, but a life not our own. We claim a distant partner who participates in our search for life whole and healed.

We reclaim the Christological symbol system when we see it as part of a community self-naming process. The images a community creates to name itself are a combination of the events that evoke the image, of the way the original viewers see the events and pass them on, and of the consciousness of those who uphold the image in the present. Images are involved in complex relational realities that are the interaction of present with past. As John Berger in *Ways of Seeing* puts it

The past is never there waiting to be discovered, to be recognized for exactly what it is . . . fear of the present leads to mystification of the past. The past is not for living in; it is a well of conclusions from which we draw in order to act . . . the past is being mystified because a privileged minority is striving to invent a history which can retrospectively justify the role of the ruling classes and such a justification can no longer make sense in modern terms. And so, inevitably, it mystifies.[20]

Patriarchal theologians have created a patriarchal Christ who mystifies the feminist quest for wholeness. Christ, however, is a complex relational image created by many. Within patriarchal culture, as within ourselves, are nonpatriarchal elements, and, though attenuated, they are not absent from the Christian tradition. We redeem Christ when we refuse to let patriarchy and its death-dealing images have the final word.

The patriarchal preoccupation with death and destruction, with alienation and the risking of death to produce life, gives us Christological symbols that divide and conquer. Symbols of a self-sacrificing perfect act of love; of God sending his son to die as a substitute for us; and of the supreme sacrifice to abstract truth of an ethical champion show us a savior crucified and dead who is the way to birth into a new abstract form of life eternal. The present, the arena of relationship, is denied. As in war, death is the terror risked and conquered by the coercive powers used to defeat its inevitablity. Salvific power is the power to die. The cross of Jesus Christ gives death the power to give life in an otherworldly, alienated future.

The cross need not, however, be a symbol that glorifies self-sacrifice and death. Death is a real experience in our lives, not because it gives us rebirth into a better life by our inviting and defying death but because it happens. Death thunders against a man, Jesus, whose fragile thread of individual life snaps. The community of Jesus' followers is empowered by his having *lived*, as prophet, healer, teacher, and friend. They give back life in remembering him with symbolic images, begetting life from life. Christ is the community remembrance of the Jesus who lived on earth. Life rejoins death, and the tension is sustained between the two because a community of living persons responds to death without defeat. Relationships give life. Jesus' followers refused to let death have the final word. The community bears witness to divine power in us, power in the passion of living persons committed to survival, to giving life to each other, and to a vision of life-as-it-can-be-lived.

In the early church's self-naming after Jesus' death, life is given through the symbols created. Minor voices, tenuous attempts at life-giving naming, sound persistently amidst the death-defying Christologies of patriarchy. The minor voices speak of the church's experiences of their own redemptive power symbolized in the stories of Jesus Christ. The voices speak of an erotic power experienced in his living with them, not in his dying for them. The healing voices persist against other sounds and speak of images that mirror feminist visions.

JESUS AS HEALING PRESENCE

One life-giving image is that of Jesus Christ as a healer. As the Klaus Seybold and Ulrich Mueller book *Sickness and Healing* demonstrates, the concern with easing suffering and restoring wholeness is not a minor biblical theme. Healing is the living Jesus' salvific power, his erotic power. Yet in our scientific age, sceptical of the miraculous, the healer is a long-neglected image. Medical science, in its preoccupation with isolating controllable, objective facts, has given us cures, but little healing. It is grounded in coercive power. In its passion to divide and conquer, medicine has focused on illness rather than on the relatedness of dis-ease. "An understanding of sickness that only deals with the personally indifferent organic and physiological process scorns, in the final analysis, the concrete person and his suffering."[21] While medicine can often cure a particular problem, it seldom restores persons to well-being and wholeness.[22]

Our experiences of suffering, of shared pain, and of our times of dis-ease belie the nonrelational presuppositions of medicine. The biblical stories of healing also belie those presuppositions and capture our experiences of suffering. The images reflect the experiences of suffering in the early church and are the community's confession of its experiences of healing. The images reveal the church's understandings of the nature of sickness and suffering, the impact of suffering on life, and the ways healing works to restore wholeness.

In the biblical stories of exorcisms, we encounter a relational view of suffering. The political realities of Roman oppression are clothed in the metaphors of demon possession. "My name is Legion; for we are many" (Mark 5:9). The church paints images of itself as possessed by powers controlling it, powers foreign to its own subjective self-determination as a community, and powers so overwhelming they are their own internalized forms of oppression.

Foreign political domination was, for Jewish understanding, *eo ipso* associated with the concept of the reign of foreign gods or demons . . . the external experience of powerlessness encountered in the face of this double oppression could be transferred to the interior.[23]

The loss of self-awareness and self-determination, the heightened self-destructive urges, and reduction of the victim to an object of total passivity or of destructive fury against others are caused by coercive powers that control and harm their victims. Demons and oppression mirror each other. When oppression is extreme enough, we feel as if we have no choices. We are forced to acquiesce to the powers, to lose ourselves, and to be possessed. We become the "Totaled Woman,"[24] obedient daughters of the patriarchy.

Biblical possessing powers relinquish their grasp only in the presence of a power they recognize as greater than their own, the power of a person centered in her/his authority, concerned with restoration and well-being, and unafraid of suffering. Faith, prayer, and direct confrontation with the powers unmask the fury of the oppressive forces and purge them. The victim is returned to a clear sense of her/himself because a new way has been opened toward wholeness.

According to Seybold and Mueller, Jesus' acts of healing are part of his proclamation of the community of God.

He did not attempt to give categories of meaning to the sick enabling them to bear the affliction more easily. Rather, he knew himself to be called to eliminate sickness and the powers standing behind it.[25]

In the healings the coming eschaton is not proclaimed by passive waiting or quiet acquiescence to suffering. Jesus' hopeful vision for the future is proclaimed by his treatment of concrete persons in pain. The threat to life is immediately before him. He responds in salvific acts of erotic power. The healing is evidence of God's power to save creation through the active care of those who find themselves confronted by suffering.

Suffering frightens people and haunts them by reminding them of their own fallibility. Biblical sickness is understood as social, but suffering removes persons from the acceptable social sphere. Suffering threatens the good status of the whole and healthy. The hemorrhaging woman is defiling and unclean; the blind are outcast beggars; and the possessed are chained amongst tombs. Dis-ease must be hidden so others are not confronted with sickness. Pain and suffering threaten the good life. To blame sickness on the victims of it is easier than to feel solidarity and compassion with the suffering. To blame the victim helps us maintain the dualisms of patriarchy and its unholy goodness.

The early church's Jesus recognizes the coercive powers behind some forms of pain. Evil is removed when it is acknowledged. Naming the powers and calling them out removes them. But Jesus is not concerned with placing ultimate blame for suffering or with protecting unholy goodness. People ask to be healed, and he heals them because he has an urgent eschatological vision of wholeness that opens him to concrete persons in his presence.[26] The church's Jesus stands with God against suffering and uses erotic power to purge illness.

The early church's Jesus is a symbol of its own experience of suffering. In the claiming of its suffering and the shattering of unholy goodness, the church felt itself made vulnerable to a new transforming reality that could heal pain and restore wholeness. Naming pain and claiming a right to their own existence opens sufferers to their own resources of energy.

A conflict of authority exists for the church in the healing stories. Where does the authority for healing lie? The miracle stories, especially in John, are used by the church as evidence of the exclusive saving power of "God's only Son." However, not all the biblical stories focus on Jesus as the source of healing. In some stories, the faith and vulnerability of the sufferer usher in the miracle, and the healer-sufferer relationship produces wholeness. Jesus is the miracle worker, not the miracle itself. He focuses divine energies toward hope and against oppressive powers the way a magnifying glass focuses light: "nowhere is this faith called 'faith in Christ.'"[27] Rather, the church responds to the way faith in God lifts the passive victim out of despair so the miracle can be worked. In Jesus, the need for faith is personified.

While healing is a proof of Jesus Christ's power and of the coming eschaton, healing does not belong exclusively to Jesus. Mark 9:38ff., Luke 9:1ff., and Acts 3:1ff. tell of others who heal. Most receive their power through Jesus Christ, but in Luke 9:49–50 other healers are recognized as part of God's salvific work. Hence, healing can have an authority outside the realm of Jesus' powers. God is at work restoring creation even in unseen corners.

The biblical stories do not resolve the ambivalence about authority. That resolution is our responsibility. The biblical images of Jesus Christ are not unifying and liberating. The images reflect the state of conflict within the communities that created them. The images cannot bind us. As a part of the community of faith we have the right to reinterpret past events and images in the light of our feminist consciousness and name those that are salvific. They are salvific when they help us find our way back to reality and each other and when they help us to transform and empower ourselves and others. They present us with possibilities for claiming what we know to be true about our existence, and the possibilities mirror back our presence to all that we love.

The healing Christological images are not the center of our faith, but they can nourish faith when they feed our power, an erotic power that helps us save the images that restore us and lead us back to each other. We redeem Christ when we recognize the images of Jesus Christ that reflect our hunger for healing wholeness and claim those images as resources for hope because we belong to a community of transformation and empowerment. Christ as healer need not be an image of exclusive power and authority. Christ is an image of shared power that works and is increased only in the sharing.

Healing reality does not emerge from a reliance on a past or future salvific event. Healing requires loving, imaginative presence here and now. Healing is active as

> gentleness swabs the crusted stump
> invents more merciful instruments
> to touch the wound beyond the wound
> . . . keeps bearing witness calmly
> against the predator, the parasite
> . . . the passion to make and make again
> where such unmaking reigns
> the refusal to be a victim
> . . . urging on
> our work, . . .
> to help the earth deliver.[28]

The feminist visions of transformation and empowerment shatter unholy goodness and redeem Christ with whole-making passions for healing. And healing is to be in each other, loving ourselves and each other fiercely into wholeness.

4. Women and Ministry: Problem or Possibility?

LETTY M. RUSSELL

Are women in ministry a problem or a possibility? Do they cause problems and difficulties for the practice of ministry in the life of the church, or do they present new possibilities for faithfulness in that ministry? This question is basic to any discussion of women and ministry. In discussing it, my contention is that women provide the opportunity for new visions of ministry and not just ecclesiastical problems.[1] And my contention is borne out by a study on women in ministry published in 1983, entitled *Women of the Cloth: A New Opportunity for the Churches.*[2]

But the question of problem or possibility is not just a matter of adding up the contributions women make to the ministry of the church and deducing the inconveniences they present for a particular committee on ordination or ministerial relations. Nor is it just a matter of arguing on biblical, historical, or theological grounds that women should be elders or deacons, ministers or priests of Word and sacrament.[3] Ultimately it is a matter of how we do our theology, of how we choose our questions, and how we arrive at answers as we think about God's call to mission and ministry in church and society.

This came home to me with particular force when I attended a meeting in Strasbourg in 1979 as a Presbyterian delegate to a World Council of Churches Consultation on Women and Ministry. I went to the meeting reluctantly; I expected that we would

Letty M. Russell is associate professor of theology at Yale University Divinity School. She was ordained in 1958 by the United Presbyterian Church, USA, and served as a pastor and educator in the East Harlem Protestant Parish for seventeen years. Dr. Russell's books include *The Future of Partnership, Growth in Partnership,* and *Becoming Human.* She is active in the Faith and Order Commission of the National Council of Churches and the World Council of Churches.

be doing the same old thing in asking women to justify themselves by proving that they are capable of representing Christ at
the altar. I was a bit tired of discussing whether I could do something I had been doing for over twenty years. And I was reluctant to travel to France in order to be an "uppity woman." That
could happen just as easily at home! Yet I hoped that something
new would happen. At the very least I would learn new things
and make new friends. And something new did happen!

Strasbourg was a new ecumenical meeting. It wasn't "just" a
women's meeting. Nor was it "just a Faith and Order (men's)
meeting!" By design, as part of the World Council Study on the
Community of Women and Men, there were eighteen women
and twelve men from fourteen countries, representing Protestant, Orthodox, Anglican, Old Catholic, and Roman Catholic
churches.[4] For the first time in my experience with such meet-
ings, women ceased to be "the problem" and the "objects" who
are studied in relation to ordination. Instead, as women and men
joined together, theology became the problem! The issue was
whether and how we could develop theological initiatives that
could make sense of the variety of ordination practices. Women
did not have to prove themselves, but theologians did! They had
to rethink together the nature of ministry as a two-class system
of the church and to clarify, not why women, but why anyone
should be ordained for life. They had to rethink the meaning of
unity at the expense of justice, for people are still talking as they
did to the women petitioning the 1929 Presbyterian General
Assembly for ordination, saying, "Don't push for ordination as
elders; it will jeopardize church union negotiations."[5] Here was
one very small hint that women could stop being a problem and
become an opportunity for a new level of shared dialogue.

This event points toward what I would like to call the "Strasbourg shift." That is, the shift in perspective and theological
discussion that comes about when women and other outsiders are
no longer a problem to be studied, but rather are participants in a
common journey to discover the meaning of life and ministry in
Christ, in the midst of diversity of nation and denomination. In
this chapter I want to explore the meaning of the "Strasbourg
shift" by looking at the underlying view of reality that leads
persons to see women and other outsiders as a problem for minis-

try, and then at possibilities for theological reflection that emerge when this perspective shifts. Lastly, I will explore an alternative vision for women in ministry that emerges when authority is exercised in community rather than over community.

SEARCHING FOR THE PROBLEM

Women and marginalized groups are viewed as a problem in the church and in seminaries because they do not fit into the dominant group or into its way of thinking. Their perspective as those who have been unseen and unheard as shapers of theology is bound to be different when it comes out of experience of non-Western cultures, or out of experiences of racial, economic, and sexist oppression. Some persons even go so far in their challenges to the theological establishment that they call for the "liberation of theology," or, "post-Christian feminism."[6] Such challenges raise fears of loss of control of the methods, integrity, and results of the theological enterprise. Questions of authority, biblical interpretation, anthropology, and ministry are only a few that become newly problematic.

PARADIGM OF DOMINATION

It would seem, however, that there is a deeper problem that may be the cause of some of the "incommunication." This is the problem of the paradigm of domination. A paradigm is a common perspective on reality made up of a particular constellation of beliefs, values, and methods.[7] The paradigm or mental picture that predominates in church and university, and in most theological research and discussion is that of a *pyramid of domination*. Consciously or unconsciously, reality is seen in the form of a hierarchy or pyramid. Ordination and every other topic are viewed in terms of super- and sub-ordination. Things are assigned a divine order, with God at the top, men next, and so on down to dogs, plants, and "impersonal" nature.[8]

In this paradigm, or way of looking at the church and world, power is undertood as domination and the "peace, unity, and purity of the church" is sought through ordering the hierarchy of doctrines. For example, the 1981 United Presbyterian General Assembly voted on the divinity of Christ in order to preserve order in the church. The particular difficulty of this approach for women and other marginal groups is that their perspectives often do not fit in the pyramid way of thought. The price of inclusion in the theological discussion about the faith of the church often turns out to be the loss of their own perspective and culture in order to do "good (orthodox) theology." Those who persist in raising questions (and raising them in perspectives that do not fit in the pyramid view) pay the price of being marginalized or pushed out of the thinking and life of the church. The extreme form of this is the emergence of so called "heretical groups," who are cut off from the possibility of mutual development and critique. Thus the attempt to enforce orthodoxy often acts as a self-fulfilling prophecy as "potential heresies" become "heresies."

The pyramid of domination is a hindrance to the peace, unity, and purity of the church, for it preserves this unity at the expense of true human diversity. Only a few are allowed into the discussion, and the very ones who were welcomed as outsiders into God's kingdom by Jesus Christ are seen as competitors to be pushed out. Concerns of such groups for justice and social change are excluded from the conversation by an appeal to orthodoxy. For instance, Sarah Cunningham reports that Allan Boesak, speaker at the 1981 United Presbyterian General Assembly from South Africa, commented on the struggle to redefine the divinity of Christ at that assembly by saying, "It may very well be a fundamental issue for many in the churches, but I have also noticed that the question of orthodoxy is always raised when we cannot face problems that overwhelm us—like power and racism and current social issues."[9]

Pyramid thinking and acting always leaves the ones at the bottom, the powerless, to pay for peace and unity. This has been happening for years and years. For instance, in five Presbyterian USA churches, women pressed for ordination in 1929 because they had been victims of the pyramid! In 1923 the Women's Board of Missions had been merged into the church without consultation with the women themselves. These women saw that they had to have a voice and a vote if they were to continue their work as witnesses to the gospel![10]

AUTHORITATIVE MINISTRY

This paradigm of domination sees authority over community as the model for orderly church life and for orderly thought about the life and mission of the church. Each of us could probably give many illustrations of the way this view of authority affects the understanding and practice of ministry. Here I would like to illustrate by showing how this view leads to interpretation of ministry as authoritative ministry.

There is general theological agreement that the biblical witness points to one calling to service for all Chirstians. By virtue of our baptism into Christ we all are called to carry out his ministry as the people of God. But from the perspective of authority over community a first- and second-class ministry tends to develop, with the clergy at the top of the pyramid as those "best" able to represent Christ on behalf of all the people. *[handwritten margin note: one call for all]*

In this view the work of Christ, traditionally described in Reformed theology as prophetic, priestly, and kingly ministry, ceases to be the work of the whole people (*laos*) and becomes the job description of the clergy. They become the ones who preach the Word, administer the sacraments, and participate in governance of the church. Ministry, viewed as authority over community and exercised from the top, in turn shapes the interpretation and function of the three-fold work of Christ: *Prophecy* is understood as the proclamation of the Word—declaring God's Word of judgment as a call to new obedience to the God-at-the-top. The *priestly* work is one of absolution, ministering to the needs of the people-at-the-bottom, and providing a means of forgiveness of sins through administering the sacraments. In the *kingly* role, clergy represent the power of God in Christ made known in the resurrection, and order the continuing life of Christ's glorified body, the church.

You are probably saying, "What is wrong with this view of authoritative ministry? What difference does it make if we see the ministry of the church as a function of authority over community?" Of course, what I have said is greatly oversimplified, and also biased. I am not claiming that this is an impossible perspective on ministry, but rather that is a very one-sided perspective that is harmful to women in ministry and to the whole people of God.[11]

Because the clergy carry out the ministry of Christ, it divides clergy from laity and inhibits the full participation of those at the bottom of the pyramid in ministry and mission. The emphasis on ministry of proclamation, absolution, and representation overshadows the meaning of Christ's ministry, which was one of service.

Lastly, women do not fit at all well into this view of ministry. One of the real problems that both women and men have with female clergy is just this—that women are not good representatives of authority, of "father right." As one local group that participated in the World Council Study on Community of Women and Men in the Church, put it:

Authority is the chief issue we recognize as we seek to understand ministry and women and men in the church. The church model of authority has been by legislation and implication a hierarchical one. It has been characterized by stereotypical masculine traits. . . . The church has tried to ordain persons to fulfill these characteristics."[12]

The paradigm of domination is alive and well in our congregations, and needs to be faced squarely, with our eyes wide open, if we are to be clear, once and for all, that the problem is not the people (women), but the paradigm itself.

ENTERTAINING THE POSSIBILITY

There are other possibilities for interpreting the reality of the church and world in which we live. One such perspective emerges from the work of feminist theology and of women in ministry. This is a perspective on reality that views women and marginal groups as full of possibility for new life and renewal.

PARADIGM OF DOXOLOGY OR PRAISE

This view of reality is a *paradigm of doxology* or praise. It looks at the world and at the church from a perspective that celebrates diversity as a way of giving glory and praise to the God of all creation. People and all of the natural world are seen as creatures of God, who praise God by seeking to become what God intends them to become as part of God's New Creation. The ordering of reality in such a paradigm is not seen as a pyramid, but as a rainbow of praise. In this view people tend to value the possibility of diversity and inclusiveness even when this breaks the pyramid of values open into a rainbow spectrum of colors, peoples, and ideas; and people are empowered for partnership.

Even chaotic diversity finds an order in this view of reality, not by subordination, but by synergy or multiplication. Different views, different cultures, races, nations, classes, and sexes come together in a spectrum that can be glimpsed in the midst of the storm of life as a sign of God's covenant with creation after the flood (Gen. 9:12). The diverse parts of God's creation refract from each other, creating a synergetic effect of more color, energy, and power.

The rainbow of doxology and cooperation presents a different possibility for the "peace, unity, and purity of the church." The unity of the church is sought in trying to reach out to the outsiders in order to discover a more inclusive consensus of shared story. This is not unlike the meaning of consensus in the original Christian community, which was a consensus in the shared story of Jesus Christ rather than doctrinal consensus.[13] Thus Paul urges unity in the congregation at Philippi by telling the story of the one who came to serve and urging that the people share that same perspective and life-style. Perhaps "having this mind" among themselves, could have led the "fathers and brethren" at the General Assembly in 1923 to celebrate the unique contribution of the Women's Board of Mission to the service of women and children around the world, rather than subordinating it and co-opting its resources.

In the story of the "Strasbourg shift" from problem to possibility we can see two small hints that there was a tentative reaching out toward expression of a changed way of doing theology. For instance, the report, *Ordination of Women in Ecumenical Perspective*, reveals that much of the work toward consensus was accomplished through the sharing of stories and questions.[14] Thus there are stories about new initiatives of women in ministry that come out of many continents and confessions. Perhaps as these stories are interpreted further in the light of the biblical story, consensus will be discovered in the many ways we live out the story of Jesus Christ, rather than in one doctrine of ministry.

In the same way some of the groups reported through the medium of a variety of questions that they had explored. In sharing questions, rather than answers, they leave the issues open so they can be lived out in each context or situation. These questions, especially when they are raised out of the experience of marginal or voiceless groups, help us to discover new ways the gospel of Christ may be challenging our views of reality.[15] Such a rainbow paradigm in theological discussion welcomes the possibility of the many new questions that arise, and may lead us to discover new clues and possibilities in the ministry of women.

SERVANT MINISTRY

The paradigm of doxology sees authority as authority-in-community.[16] This is a model for ordering church life, and for orderly thought about the life and mission of the church that would have many implications for the practice of ministry. Here I would like to illustrate by showing how this view leads to interpretation of servant ministry in contrast to the authoritative ministry.

There are many ways to come to theological consensus about the work of Christ. As we have seen, Paul himself celebrates the mystery of Christ's humanity and divinity in a hymn of praise to the one who "emptied himself, taking the form of a servant" (Phil. 2:7). For it is the story, not the creeds, that makes God's action in serving us plausible. In words of Dorothee Soelle: "I don't as they put it believe in God, but to him I can't say no as hard as I try."[17] Symbols of slavery or servanthood so often used in the New Testament continue to evoke strong images and experiences of domination and involuntary subordination. Yet the scandal of the words is the heart of the gospel story (Matt. 23:11). The Lord who voluntarily became a servant, who suffered out of love for others, has called us to do likewise.

This understanding of ministry as service is common in every Christian tradition. For instance, the agreed upon statement on ministry drafted by Roman Catholic and Anglican theologians at Canterbury in 1975 stressed the servant character of the ordained person who is servant of both Christ and church.[18]

Paul and the gospel writers had a very different pattern of

service in mind than the one to which we are accustomed. Here we have a description of service as a form of empowerment for and with others. This is a form of voluntary self-giving, not involuntary servitude by those considered less-than-whole-selves. This is service seen as a way that God's gifts multiply for all creation, rather than a way human beings are reduced to fit their "proper place" (at the bottom).

The work of Christ as prophet, priest, and king looks quite different when it is seen in this rainbow perspective of empowerment for servant ministry. No one has a corner on service, and no one has a pinnacle to stand on. It is a vocation we can all share, according to the variety of our gifts. Authority in community seeks the recognition of gifts wherever they emerge in the community among both laity and clergy, praising God for diversity rather than fearing it.

Servant prophecy is understood as the way the church speaks the truth out of love. For the prophetic word is one that emerges out of solidarity with people. Prophecy requires sufficient solidarity and sharing of life so that it becomes possible for us to share in the prophetic gift of knowing when to speak words of comfort and when to speak judgment. Such words may multiply the gift of "prophetic imagination" among us so that our changed consciousness and action leads us to praise God by living out God's intention for our lives and world.[19] Such servant prophecy is a call to solidarity with God-in-our midst.[20]

Servant priesthood is a form of shared suffering with Christ in the midst of those who suffer. Ministry with those at the bottom, the victims of an economic, political, and cultural way of life that benefits a few at the expense of many. Social as well as personal sin is lifted up to God in the breaking of bread and in the cup of cold water, as we learn to become what Lora Gross calls the "embodied people of God in the world."[21]

Servant kingship is particularly difficult, because we are accustomed to rulership as top-down dominating authority. In fact, it is best to speak of Christ as liberator and not king. The three aspects of Christ's ministry could then be described as prophecy, suffering, and liberation. The metaphor of kingship seems more suited to the paradigm of the pyramid. But what does it mean in the rainbow paradigm? Perhaps, without the refraction of meaning that comes from the two ideas, servanthood and lordship together, there is no way to understand servant ministry as a gift of God's Spirit, a form of liberation empowerment that orders the continuing life of Christ's glorified body as a community of care and of creativity. For as Beverly Harrison has said, the awesome truth is that "we have the power through acts of love or lovelessness literally to create one another."[22]

This view of the ministry of the church as a function of Christ's authority in community through solidarity, suffering, and empowerment may also seem one-sided. But at least it promotes partnership in ministry among the whole people of God. Furthermore, it is not as utopian as it sounds. Authority in community is rooted in the life-style of the one who came "not to be served but to serve and to give his life as a ransom for many" (Mark 10:45). It is also lived out in the ministry of many women. It expresses the experience of women, and of not a few men, in ministry, who discover that authority exercised in community may appear to be inefficient and messy but is the way to serve and be served, with respect for the "human rights" and "creature rights" of all God's creation.

TOWARD AUTHORITY IN COMMUNITY

A theological understanding of authority in community is essential to the life and health of women in ministry because the conflicting views of authority and the exercise of ministry often are at the root of the problems of acceptance in the church, and of self-acceptance. For instance, Barbara Brown Zikmund has identified three common concerns that emerge as "women in ministry face the eighties: credibility, rivalry, and calling."[23] All three are issues of authority. In a paradigm of domination, credibility is difficult or impossible to achieve because the model of domination is male patriarch (human and divine).

Rivalry increases because women compete with one another to emulate the oppressor and join their male colleagues in competing to reach the top of the pyramid by exercising power as domination. Calling is always in doubt for women, because some churches consider them incapable of representing Christ at the altar. It is also questionable because ordination into a privileged class of clergy seems to perpetuate the subordination of the laity and is likely to be uncomfortable for those who find themselves playing at the "Herr Pastor" role. In any case sexism continues to perpetuate inequities between women and men in ministry as women remain marginal to what has long been understood as an exclusively masculine role.[24]

In a paradigm of authority in community there is no easy resolution of these concerns, but at least there is the possibility of acting and thinking in ways that model the servant ministry of Christ. Authority is not something to be either embraced or avoided in the search for credibility. Women have been taught to fear and avoid power and authority, and now they have a double aversion to this role because of the feminist ideal of shared leadership. Yet women in ministry do not need to fear power. For power as ability to implement can be exercised as empowerment of others rather than domination of others. And authority can be authority in community where credibility or the right to exercise power is acknowledged as an enabling gift for the ministry of the whole community of faith.

In this sense, one's credibility is a gift of the Spirit of God which makes possible the upbuilding of the community for service in the world. Rivalry between women, and between women and men seeking advancement in their profession, can be transformed into valued diversity by a perspective that welcomes different contributions to the whole. Vocation as God's call to freedom and service in a witnessing community can become an expression, not of privilege or class status, but of the calling of every Christian. Enabling the whole people of God to grow by functioning as the "Mother" of a congregation may be a way of responding to God's call as women seek to carry out their ministries in Christian community.[25]

CHANGING THE PARADIGM

Such shifts in perspective call for an ever growing sense of self-worth as a child of God, and self-identity as a participant in the ministry and life-style of Jesus of Nazareth. But the shift itself is crucial for women and men, and for the church, to say nothing of our world of domination, oppression, and suffering. As Elizabeth Fiorenza wrote in 1975: "The very character of the hierarchical-patriarchal church structure has to be changed if women are to attain their place and full authority within the Church and theology."[26]

The more women study the past traditions of female and male leadership in the church, the more they become convinced that, at root, it is a new paradigm of reality and, therefore, of ministry that is called for. Patriarchy is not only a way of life that functions to justify the domination of all those marginal to the self-interest of dominant males, but also is a "conceptual trap" that can explain logically, consistently, and with endless documentation just why women, foreigners, slaves, physically handicapped, the poor, and many more, are inferior and incapable of bearing authority over others.[27]

Interestingly, when we change the paradigm to authority in community, the paradigms for ministry are much more in line with the New Testament idea of ministry as sharing in Christ's ministry of service and sacrifice. There are many paradigms of ministry in the New Testament, for this sharing in service emerged in different forms and ways according to the needs of different congregations. Our various confessional traditions of ministry each have picked out particular paradigms and made them normative. But the paradigm of the rainbow would lead us to recognize that the different titles of apostle, evangelist, prophet, teacher, shepherd, priest, and more are all descriptions of gifts for ministry and do not necessitate only one form or order of ministry (1 Cor. 12).[28]

In order to move in this direction, some women choose to remain as lay persons, and some have *no choice*. Others join the ever-growing number of women clergy. All who work in the church, however, have to cultivate a double vision of reality. The structures in which they work are still structures of authority over community, and in order to survive in them they must analyze and understand how they function. Here support groups of women in ministry who help one another understand what seems to be happening are essential. At the same time those who see ministry in the perspective of authority in community will also need others who can help cultivate these alternative visions and search for ways of living out of the rainbow perspective on ministry.

DEVELOPING A SYNERGETIC PROCESS

The energy to sustain a double vision and work toward changing the paradigm of ministry can be discovered in the midst of communities of faith. Just as the loaves and fishes multiplied to make possible Jesus' feeding of the five thousand, there is a continuing multiplication factor wherever the gifts of God's love are shared in community. If we begin in every circumstance to value the people with whom we work, it will become easier for us to find the gifts they have that can be shared with others. While resisting the stereotypes and attitudes that seek to place them in a small and lower niche in the pyramid, women can still look for ways of increased power and authority in community, promoting unity through welcoming others to the Lord's table rather than "fencing them out."

In one church a woman pastor was visited by a laywoman who wanted to reach out to the physically challenged persons in the church and community. The pastor welcomed this idea and helped the parishioner develop a Committee on Ministry with the Aging and Disabled (COMAD). Over half of the committee members were themselves physically challenged and welcomed the opportunity to plan for a ramp-fund campaign, educational programs, and worship services. In only a year, half of the money had been raised for the renovations and modifications to the church buildings; worship services had been led by physically challenged persons; and the youth group had written and presented a play to raise the consciousness of the congregation. In spite of old ways of thinking—"We don't want to destroy the historic beauty of our building. Why do we need a ramp when so few people in wheelchairs attend church?"—the synergetic process was at work, breaking down physical and mental barriers.[29]

OVERCOMING THE PINNACLE COMPLEX

Probably the greatest temptation for women and men in ministry is the "pinnacle complex." It is not accidental that Jesus' temptations carried him to the pinnacle of the temple, and that Luke 4:1–13 highlights this religious temptation by placing it at the end of the three. In Jesus' own life, as in the life of clergypersons, the need for religious credibility and authority tempts persons to clothe themselves in the sacred. If it can be shown by dress, sex, or dramatic actions that you are specially chosen and protected by God, then the many problems of uncertainty and inadequacy can be concealed, and the problems of stubborn or unruly church officials will be overcome. Of course, they may not be as great a temptation for women clergy because they simply do not possess the "sacred masculinity" required to bring this off in our male-oriented church and society. The writers of *Women of the Cloth* underline this situation by quoting Wilbur Bock's study of the status and role of clergywomen in 1967: "According to Bock, the ministry 'has not only been defined as masculine, but as "sacredly" masculine. The father figure, a prominent feature of Christianity, is also a prominent ingredient in the image of the clergy.' "[30]

Nevertheless, the structures of human sin are such that in any organization there is a tendency to return to the pyramid structure of relationship if people do not intentionally organize their church life with "checks and balances" like John Calvin, or with some other way of overcoming the pinnacle complex. One way to overcome it is to look constantly for ways of sharing the work and perspective of those at the bottom of any organizational ladder. If you do not want to tempt God by trying to fool yourself and others into thinking God has special care for you by virtue of your status, just spend time sharing the work and perspectives of the church secretary or janitor. For these people, clergy do not "walk on water" or ride on the "wings of angels." Rather clergy are seen as "part-time workers" who go home early, sleep late, and call on the others to take care of things.

According to Jean Baker Miller, the key to overcoming the view of power and authority as domination is to cultivate "temporary inequality."[31] In relationships of temporary inequality, the subordinate persons are in that position until they learn, grow, or develop so that they become equal to or better than the temporarily dominant persons. Such is the relationship of parent/child, student/teacher, and it should be the relationship of clergy/parishioners. But our relationships in society and the church are usually ones of "permanent inequality" in which people are defined according to certain characteristics of birth such as race, sex, class, nationality, or religion and placed in categories of domination and subordination. Categories like clergy and laity are usually permanent and even have a theology of indelibility to "prove it." Regardless of what we say about ministry as a function, we are still placed in a position of permanent superiority in the life of the church. In this sense ordination becomes an indelible mark of caste rather than the recognition of spiritual gifts for a particular ministry of the church.

The first step in overcoming this is to recognize that the particular position held is to be functional for the life and mission of the church. This might well mean that the church would need other types of ministry at other times, and that you also might be in very different types of service, in or outside the church, at various times of your life. The second step is that of cultivating "temporary inequality" in the life of the church, seeking ways to work our way out of jobs and to become invisible in the church as others discover their gifts of ministry.

One small illustration of this happened to a minister of education in the New Haven, Connecticut, area. She decided to plan the Vacation Church School as an intergenerational event. By including the elderly in baking cookies and serving refreshments, welcoming teenagers as program assistants, calling persons who do not normally have time to teach or share talents of music, art, or story, she developed a teaching and learning community. As the school got underway she enjoyed walking around and visiting the children and teachers at work. One day she fell into conversation with a little girl who asked, "What do you do around here, anyway?"[32] Perhaps some of us are worried that our church will fire us if we work ourselves out of a job, but the fact remains that the pinnacle complex can only be avoided when all persons discover that they are so special in God's sight that they do not even need to test out that love by climbing over others!

FINDING SUBVERSIVE POSSIBILITIES

Even with these various attempts at changing the paradigm of authority, there will always be need for subverting the pyramid of domination because of its power in our lives and institutions. In his book *Authority*, Richard Sennett points out that one can increase democracy and participation in an organization even when the structures are paternalistic and hierarchical, by disrupting the links in the top-down chain of command.[33] This type of action may appear to cause trouble, but it results in challenging and opening up organizational structures and attitudes so that people are better able to see the way things function and to understand what is happening.

Authority of doxology which celebrates diversity and seeks unity through inclusion of cooperating groups may happen in only small ways in our lives, but it can provide a critical perspective on reality that leads to the questioning of established rules, procedures, and forms of status—and possibly to the renewal of the church. Authority of domination always works through a chain of command from top to bottom and it works most effectively when the right to exercise power is unquestioned, and the structures of organization are assumed but not understood. If we are to avoid either anarchy or co-option into the system of domination, we need to develop strategies of disruption that reflect our double vision.

Sennett suggests a few strategies that we might want to try.[34] First he suggests that we require the *active voice* so that any order that says, "It has been decided," has to be explained in terms of who and why, so that the decision becomes questionable. Discuss the *assumed categories* into which persons are placed and the way *decisions* might be carried out differently. The last two suggestions are particularly important in the life of the church. Disrupt the chain of command by *role exchange* so that those in charge take on "subordinate tasks" through rotation and temporary inequality. I use to do this in my church in East Harlem by sharing in tasks of cleaning and typing so that the janitor and secretary could share in teaching, workshop, and calling. *Challenge the assumption* that something is really helpful and "nourishing." Paternalistic church structures promise nurture and care, but often leave people dependent. The service people prefer is that which helps them gain the ability to care for themselves, and sometimes direct aid becomes a way of increasing dependence and subordination.

Finding ways to subvert the church into being the church is both difficult and risky. One area which seems to open up a great deal of reaction and fear is the use of inclusive language for God and human beings. Language both describes and conceals the structures of social reality. When language is challenged, the reality it represents is also challenged. If the generic use of "man" to include "woman" is challenged, then structures that include women in subordination to men are also questioned. If God transcends both masculine and feminine traits and yet can be imaged as both Father and Mother, then the privilege of the clergy in representing the Patriarch is questioned. Each time we try to make language of worship more inclusive we find out the depth of resistance to any disruption of the pyramid. Yet sometimes such simple things as reading the story of the Prodigal Son and Father as the Prodigal Daughter and Mother may open persons' eyes to the wealth of insight they are missing by such a narrow perspective on God and world. (Luke 15:11–32).[35]

It is not easy to move toward authority in community within a church of authority over community, yet this is a journey that is important for the well being of all the members of Christ's church. The various clues for this journey—changing the paradigm, developing a synergetic process, overcoming the pinnacle complex, and finding subversive possibilities—are simply invitations to women and men in ministry to seek out new visions of humanity and of the church that offer the possibility of partnership among women and men, laity and clergy.

All this talk about the problems and possibilities of women in ministry is not a coverup for saying that men are the problem, although of course, they sometimes are. It is a way, however, of saying that domination is a human problem called sin. In the light of this problem, we need a "Strasbourg shift" in our paradigms of authority. The church has no business continuing to order its life and thought in pyramids of domination. Supposedly we left those pyramids in Egypt long ago! Why not "let Pharaoh go" and try the rainbow for a change?

For years women have thought in rainbows. Why else would Professor Henry Higgins (of "My Fair Lady" fame), and every other professor, always have to "straighten up the mess that's inside?" It is time to stop apologizing and feeling inadequate and to live out this affirmative vision of ministry. For God has put the rainbow in the midst of the storm to show that God cares! And God said: "When the bow is in the clouds, I will look upon it and remember the everlasting covenant between God and every living creature of all flesh that is upon the earth" (Gen. 9:16).

II. PERSONAL AND CULTURAL ISSUES

5. American Women and Life-Style Change

NANETTE M. ROBERTS

In 1953, at the age of twenty, I graduated from college. My working-class family and friends were pleased but hardly impressed. Their constant question, directed to my mother, was, "Well, that's fine, but when is she going to get married?" Four years later, married to their satisfaction and my own and teaching at a major university, the question from them and my mother was, "But when are you going to have a baby?"

Despite the many changes in women's lives, life-styles, and legal situation today, these same questions and assumptions confront most women. About ninety percent of all women marry at some time in their lives, and most have children or raise some other woman's children. Thus when examining the life-styles of modern women, it is still to women's experience with marriage and motherhood that we must look most carefully and most critically to determine the real parameters of life-style change.

This fact should not surprise us, since acculturation toward marriage and motherhood begins early in virtually every girl's life. As sociologist Jessie Bernard observed, using the term "prime time" to describe women's late teens and early twenties,

Regardless of her interests and concerns, the prime-time world is organized to propel [a woman] . . . on to marriage. The norms are like cilia, moving her in that direction. If . . . almost everyone takes it for granted

---

Nanette M. Roberts is general secretary of the Division of Higher Education and the American Missionary Association of the United Church of Christ Board for Homeland Ministries; formerly she was secretary for Family Life and Women's Issues of that agency. She earned her Ph.D. in English and American Literature from New York University, where she held a Woodrow Wilson National Dissertation Fellowship in Women's Studies.

that marriage and motherhood are the first order of the day, it becomes all but impossible to do anything different.[1]

The process is undergirded by powerful, organized groups— political and often religious—who extol the excellence of the patriarchal family both for itself and for its consonance with public order, the American way, and the will of God. The age at first marriage is slowly increasing, but most women make their decision to marry without enough maturity to evaluate the institution or to understand that they may need to adapt it to their changing lives.

That women are moving away from or transforming marriage and motherhood to a considerable degree is the story of our time, a story fraught with revolutionary potential. The changes which have come about have depended primarily on two externals: the development of an economic system which, over the last several decades, has created service and clerical jobs for workers who will accept low pay—for example, women—and on the medical and legal breakthroughs which make relatively reliable and safe birth control and abortion available. The so-called liberation of women is being articulated and debated by social, political, and religious theorists; its basis lies in the realms of economic and technological change.

We will examine here several significant aspects of the lifestyles of American women, making an effort to deal with women young and old, with rich and poor, with white women and women of color. The pluralism of American women, like that of the culture, poses a formidable caution against generalization. Many older women reflect a vanishing world, but the women they have mothered bear their mark. In a society whose average age is increasing steadily, and where three-fifths of those over sixty-five are women, the lives of older women deserve consideration. They too are affected by life-style change, and their lives provide both cautions and promises to young women. Women of color, still a numerical minority, share experiences common to all women, but they belong to groups whose men are also discriminated against and often disadvantaged.[2] Thus they do not have the protection of a dominant-group partner or parent, which most white women have for at least some of their lives.

Access to and acceptance of birth control, abortion, and the job market have brought over forty million American women into the paid labor force. But American women still marry at about age twenty-two, and millions see marriage as *the* necessary element in their lives. Similarly, many women who remain child-free until their thirties and forties are now producing a baby "boomlet," becoming mothers at ages when their own mothers became or expected to become grandmothers.

Thus the major themes of women's lives are still variations upon marriage and motherhood, but many younger women are changing the time frame within which those events occur, delaying marriage and/or motherhood, and combining the traditional role of wife and mother with a commitment to work outside the home that their own mothers did not have as young women. The mothers, meanwhile, are often rediscovering the world of work in their own midlife. Variations on themes can—and sometimes do—make a new song.

In attempting to describe the life-styles of so diverse a group, we will focus on three salient areas of change: woman's self-image, her experience with family (marriage, nonmarriage, divorce, separation, motherhood, and alternative intimate relationships), and her developing relationships to the world of paid labor. Finally, we will look at the theological and religious questions these new issues raise.

All efforts at description try to arrest for examination a reality which is ever changing: today's single woman may be a married woman or mother tomorrow; the secure suburban housewife of today may be a displaced homemaker next week; today's widow or divorcée may ultimately find herself in a multiperson household with other single-parents and children, or may remarry into a stepfamily household. Thus description falsifies a changing reality by stopping it for analysis; the reader must remember that the reality is in constant flux.

WOMEN'S SELF-IMAGE

Several obvious changes in women's lives confront us daily. Despite the recent defeat of the Equal Rights Amendment (ERA), women are increasingly visible, increasingly aware of the nature of their struggle, more angry, more determined, and more willing to speak out than at any time in the recent past. Issues like rape, wife beating, and abortion are out of the closet, and many political, special interest, and labor organizations now assist women politically and economically. Although probably only a minority of women actually belong to or actively support these groups, their work affects us all, providing avenues of appeal, change, or protest, or monitoring governmental action. They have raised women's and girls' sense of their own value, an important prerequisite to positive life-style change.

Media change has been particularly important. Women and men now see "women's vote" polled or discussed seriously, and women's issues enlarged beyond traditional concerns to issues as diverse as career planning, sexual harassment, violence and rape, abortion, or women in sports. Simultaneously, women have begun to appear as serious reporters and media personalities, and newspapers, television, and textbooks are moving, however slowly, toward inclusive language and coverage. For the scholar, women's studies has become a respectable area of academic inquiry.

All these changes raise women's consciousness, helping them realize the value of their lives. More importantly, they help women realize that they and their experience cannot be covered by the term *man* and *mankind,* because women's lives are, in markedly important ways, different from those of men. Our growing psychological and intellectual recognition of that difference is a major factor in life-style change.

An important change in women's self-evaluation appears in their changing attitudes toward their most personal physical possession, their own bodies. Until very recently little was expected of women physically but that they be pretty, slim, and sexually attractive to men. Needless to say, to be significant, they had also to be young, preferably white or with Caucasian features. Exercise and diet served primarily to enhance these goals, and women were barred by custom and self-selection from games and competitions that men and boys took for granted. Women's sports, where they existed at all, were rarely taken seriously, or given real financial support.

Today much has changed. Laws supporting educational equity for women's sports are beginning to be felt, although legal action is often required to put them into effect.[3] Women have in fact come a long way since 1967, when Kathy Switzer entered the Boston Marathon as K. Switzer, permitting the organizers to assume that she was male. Women today run the marathon in times at which men were winning it only a few decades ago, and women in sports are now treated with considerable respect.

More importantly, women of all ages are taking themselves and their bodies seriously, reflecting concern for fitness and proper diet. To be sure, the physical and emotional effects of the old restrictions are still with us, and anorexia and bulimia still distort the lives of women and girls who deny their own body type, often in search of a commercially exploited emaciation idealized as beautiful. But it is becoming increasingly acceptable for women to consider a wide range of body types satisfying, and to aim for strength as well as shapeliness as acceptable goals.

As more women seek greater physical control over their environments by developing their bodies to cope with challenge and stress, they also come to control other aspects of their physical lives. Movements like women's health collectives show our changing attitudes not only toward our bodies but also toward the physicians who monitor them, and many women see signs of improvement in the behavior of doctors who, for far too long, assumed an unquestioned patriarchal authority. The patronizing attitudes that often governed the medical profession's treatment of women in pregnancy and menopause, or in their search for birth control or sterilization, have begun to go the way of the cold speculum or the one-sided use of first names or "dear" in our dialogue.

For many women, the right to reproductive freedom through abortion rests on new assumptions about their autonomy over their own bodies and their life space. Rape crisis hotlines, centers for abused or battered women, attention paid to sexual harassment, and new attitudes toward childbirth and midwifery indicate a raised consciousness about physical autonomy. Many feminists and theologians are moving toward a sexual ethic based on mutual consent as the only basis for sexual, procreational, or social behavior, in marked opposition to the female subordination to husband traditionally preached by our major religions.

With their increased awareness of their actual physical capabilities, a growing number of women emerge as models of psychological and physical independence. It can be hoped that women in general will eventually feel increasingly capable of physical competence and the enhanced emotional autonomy that results. Yet the often negative realities of female life remain. Virtually all women, like their mothers before them, will always live with a constant awareness of vulnerability, the physical and cultural disadvantages relative to men that keep them subject to rape, abuse, sexual harassment, or intimidation.[4] Only rarely fully conscious of these fears, women nonetheless build into their behavior at a very early age responses to and defenses against physical victimization.

Still, the changes in women's attitudes toward their bodies are encouraging, with far-reaching effects for young and old. Just as the beauty of women of color and of older women is being recognized, so many postmenopausal women refuse to accept the notions that assign them to life's dust heap. As our ideals become less stereotypical, more and more women insist upon being judged upon their own terms physically, intellectually, and behaviorally.

This growing and positive sense of self underlies the decision of an increasing number of women to retain their birth names even after marriage, the life change which has historically been marked by the loss of their most intimate psychological possession, their name. Yet these women are still few in number; for every woman who goes into marriage with changed expectations and behavior, many, many more still seek the conventional life. Women's experience with marriage and family—historically their primary life choices—is now simultaneously the cornerstone of tradition and the major focus of life-style change.

WOMEN'S LIFE-STYLES

In 1979, Census Bureau demographer Paul Glick testified before a congressional committee. In his "The Future of the American Family," Glick made several important observations. He noted the life-style changes then apparent: the increase in longevity for both sexes, women's shift away from the large numbers of children that their mothers had favored, the rising divorce rate, the increased participation in the paid labor force, and the postponement of first marriage to a median age for males of 24.0 years and of 21.6 for females.[5]

Glick reported that in 1977 nearly two million adults were living together without being married, "an eighty percent increase over their 1,046,000 counterparts in 1970,"[6] but observed that this figure was still only 2 percent of all households.[7] He documented the rapid increase in the number of young adults living alone (an increase of 56 percent between 1970 and 1977), one-fourth of them as a result of separation or divorce, but observed that "a substantial majority" of them consisted of male singles. With the new tendency to delay first marriages, Glick predicted that "unless the cohort of women now in their twenties has an unusually large number of late marriages, the chances are that 6 percent—or even 7 or 8 percent—of them will go through life without ever becoming married,"[8] a rate of nonmarriage about twice that of the cohort born only twenty years earlier. Despite these changes, Glick showed that about 87 percent of all persons still lived in households headed by either a married couple (77 percent) or by a single parent (10 percent). Single parenthood was closely associated with educational level; the greatest increase in this category at that time was in families where one or both parents had not completed high school.[9]

Glick then suggested that cohabitation "for at least a period of several months" among young adults would probably become more common in the next decade, but declined to conjecture how much or whether the "*lifetime* proportion of unmarried couples"[10] would also rise. He suggested that delaying first marriage might promise somewhat enhanced marital stability and, recognizing the increasing presence of women in the paid labor force, stressed the imperative need for good quality childcare, and for flextime or part-time work schedules. Finally, he declared that "during the next decade or two social pressure may . . . diminish for both a working mother and her husband to be employed on a full-time basis."[11]

The 1980 Census confirms many of the trends Glick described. Because of divorce, the single-parent family is our fastest growing family type, and nearly half of all black children live in a single-parent home.[12] Women-headed families are far more likely to live below the poverty line than are families headed by men, and the effects of class, race, and marital status are everywhere apparent in women's life-styles. But nine out of ten persons still live in households headed by two adults or by a single parent, and the age at first marriage continues up slightly (at 24.8 years for males, 22.3 for females); 10 percent of the population may never marry at all.

Perhaps the most important statement about marriage and women was made by Jessie Bernard over a decade ago, when she observed that every marriage is in fact two marriages, his and hers.[13] The observation still holds, for the vast majority of women, despite steady advances in educational level, continue to marry men who are older, bigger, stronger, better educated, and better paid than they themselves are. All of these attributes are indicators of power and respect in our society. Thus marriage puts women into an initially disadvantaged position on several scores, and the socialization of women and girls, which pushes them inexorably toward marriage and motherhood, functions to make them subordinate partners in a patriarchal institution.

Men and women enter marriage and all other relationships strongly conditioned by the values of their own families and culture. The famous Broverman study of 1971 asked health care professionals to describe the characteristics of emotionally healthy women, men, and adults. Its results illustrated that only a decade ago, illogic, emotionalism, and dependence were considered typical of adult women by the very helpers to whom they turned in emotional crisis.[14] The Broverman study viewed adult women as grown-up children, preferably charming, pleasing, and delightful, but children nonetheless. Depression and masochism were also thought characteristic of female personalities, and although isolated voices like that of Karen Horney argued that these conditions resulted from the lifelong experience of dependency upon others for emotional, economic, and social status and security, very few in the professional establishment were convinced.[15] Such attitudes, all degrading to women, are part of modern women's cultural legacy. Meanwhile, women of color carry white society's disparagement of their race as well as their sex.

Women have traditionally coped with inequality and subordination by learning to charm and to please, and often to manipulate the men upon whom they depend for support and status.[16] But their feelings of dependency and devaluation are not without factual basis. Married women, especially those who stay home and have children, are *in fact* dependent upon their husbands for status, economic security, love and affection, food, clothing, and recreation. Even if women work outside the home, their husbands are usually the major providers of all these necessities. Thus many married women really are dependent, and internalize habits of thought and self-evaluation destructive of the autonomy upon which full personhood depends.

Motherhood offers similar difficulties in conventional marriage. There is real ego-stress in women's adjustment to the cooption of their bodies and life space, a disruption which continues for most women well past the childhood of their children. Any mother who loses needed sleep, relaxation, or career opportunities because of the needs of her children may frequently feel that even well loved children are the enemy. Anatomy may not be destiny, but motherhood has traditionally imposed on most women far more restrictions, responsibilities, and burdens of guilt than fatherhood has on most men. Perhaps because the mother is usually blamed if the child turns out badly, most women carry a far greater level of both the physical and the emotional childrearing tasks than do their husbands.

More importantly, they carry the society's assumption that, in the last analysis, parenthood is a woman's responsibility. Whether in the areas of contraception, child custody, or the search for child care, it is the woman who is expected—and who usually concurs in that expectation—to solve the problem. However few children she has, the mother is occupied far more than the father with child care. If, as is predicted, one-half of all children will soon live for at least a time in a single-parent (usually female-headed) family, we see the real overload of responsibility placed on mothers.[17] Without good quality child care, flextime, and employment policies that reflect the needs of women with children, there will be no equality for women, neither economic nor attitudinal.

That American women have responded to these realities as

forthrightly as they have constitutes a real revolution in family and personal life. Women are also limiting the period of time during which they give birth. These are truly radical changes, giving women a degree of control over their lives never before experienced.

Because marriage and motherhood have depended (and in great measure still depend) upon a profound male-female inequality of power, status, and economic reward, any critique is bound to be opposed by powerful elements within our society. The changes in women's life-styles in the past twenty years have evoked an extraordinarily defensive and effective response from individuals and from political and religious groups. The successful attack on the ERA spearheaded by Phyllis Schlafly—the symbol of the happy housewife and her resistance to legal equality— testifies to the rejection by many women of any critique of the life-styles toward which they were nurtured. And it must be remembered that the vast majority of women marry, have children, and, if their marriages end, often remarry. Thus despite the contradictions inherent in the marital relationship, it is a major part of female experience, and great numbers seek no change.

The experience of dependence in marriage, coupled with the major responsibility of parenthood, is the inevitable consequence of women's acculturation, her life experience, and our economic system.[18] Our culture has never been pro-woman and, for all its posturing, it is not pro-family. Women who seek to find alternatives to the traditional roles often find their efforts blocked by reality. When a husband's job promotion, evaluation, or respect at work depend upon his performing in traditional ways, and when he brings home one dollar for every fifty-nine cents she earns if she works outside the home,[19] few women dare jeopardize the family's security by asserting that housework is also a full-time job, or that full-time work is full-time work whatever the salary level. The economic reality of job discrimination in the work place tends to block women's aspirations, to keep them from seeing their needs as equal in importance to those of husband or family. A marriage with a second place in it cannot be egalitarian.

Both women and men are increasingly aware of these issues.

Whether prompted by a new realism or, as some have charged, a new narcissism, both sexes are turning to other life-styles. Today millions marry and remarry, but millions also divorce, cohabit, or remain voluntarily single or childfree. Their life-styles may well constitute a massive indictment of traditional marriage and parenthood and the assumptions upon which they rest, and may in time force wide-ranging changes within those essential but difficult experiences.

The rising acceptance of divorce is of considerable significance. About 38 percent of all first marriages end in divorce; the divorce rate in second marriages is somewhat higher. Rates vary in different parts of the country and, to some extent, with religious affiliation.[20] Whether we have in fact achieved the practice popularly termed "serial marriage" seems dubious, since one or two marital partners over an extended life span hardly constitute a series, and for most persons one marital partner is still the norm. Certainly, this high level of divorce indicates a widespread movement away from the concept of "till death do us part." We now have an increasing number of persons, particularly children, for whom divorce and remarriage seem normal parts of life. In the first long-term studies of children of divorce, the children voice a strong preference for one, lasting marriage; their practice, however, suggests that in fact they are somewhat more inclined to divorce than children of never-divorced parents.[21] Consequently, it is probable that divorce, single parenting, remarriage, and stepparenting will figure prominently in the life-styles of a significant number of women.

Our present divorce rate is the highest ever recorded in the United States, and divorce, like marriage, is very different for women and men. Divorce creates a far greater economic downturn for women, and often brings the emotional stress of single parenting. Still there appears to be little rejection of marriage: five out of six men and three out of four women remarry after divorce. The differing rates of remarriage probably reflect the male's greater need for marriage, his greater freedom (men rarely take custody of their children),[22] and his greater earning power (some studies suggest that as many as 70 percent of women on welfare are there because their ex-husbands do not fulfill their responsibilities for child support).[23] The statistics also reflect the double standard of aging in our culture, which often considers middle-aged women too old for remarriage but men desirable marriage partners at virtually any age. Eventually, statistics may also document women's lessening economic need for marriage as the job market continues to welcome them.

The experience of black women with divorce is quantitatively different from that of women in other racial groups. The divorce rate among blacks has grown to more than double that of white and Hispanics within the last ten years: in 1979 there were 104 divorced black women for every 1,000 blacks in the population; in 1980 the rate was 257 per 1,000. Comparable figures for white women jumped from 56 divorced women per 1,000 in 1970 to 110 in 1980, and for Hispanics from 81 per 1,000 to 133. (Divorced men appear at lower figures per 1,000 because of their higher rate of remarriage.)[24]

These differences undoubtedly reflect the lower earning power of blacks and Hispanics, with its consequent stress on the male's self-image and on the marriage itself. It is therefore no surprise that black women are heavily represented among single-parent family heads, and are more likely to live below the poverty line than are white women.

For poor women of all races, government policy as represented in the Aid for Families with Dependent Children program often effects the breakup of poor families by demanding that the father be absent before the mother and children can receive help. Welfare supports women-headed families at a subsistence level, while making it almost impossible for the women to find work or childcare. Such programs for women and children, however inadequate, may assist men to pass their economic and moral responsibilities off to the larger society, while single-parent women carry the major economic and emotional burden of family life.

Although marriage and motherhood are still the norm for most women, the number of households headed by persons living alone is enormous in absolute terms. Two out of three such households are now headed by single women over fifty-five, often women who are divorced, separated, or widowed.[25] Since the typical married woman is widowed at fifty-six, some experience with singleness awaits most women, and they need to be prepared. Meanwhile the percentage of women aged twenty to twenty-five who have not yet married—and may never do so—now approaches 15 percent, a 50 percent increase since 1970 and a marked change from the experience of their own mothers, who were among the youngest brides in our history.[26]

Many women are opting against marriage, or at least building their lives on the assumption that marriage is by no means their foremost goal. Others are choosing to be voluntarily childless, or *childfree* as they may prefer; still others are taking advantage of legal changes that permit single women to become mothers through adoption. In life-style changes of this kind we see, as might be expected, a preponderance of middle-class, relatively well educated women, in part because such life-styles necessitate a relatively comfortable income.

The opportunity for young singles to live alone frequently results from the entry of their mothers into the paid labor force. In the past, young adults often lived in the family home, and contributed to it economically. Now their mothers are often in the paid labor force, and the children are freed to live more independently. With the economic turbulence of the last several years, however, many young persons have been forced to return home at least temporarily, a phenomenon dubbed by the popular press the "refilled nest syndrome," in contrast to the famous "empty nest" depression that was at one time considered virtually inevitable for mothers of grown children. Interestingly, as other options for use of their abilities became available to the mothers, the empty nest setback has become far less common.[27]

With the changes in real estate and banking practices effected by feminists, single women can now buy property in their own names; many own houses, apartments, or businesses. Still others live, for shorter or longer periods, in multiperson households of primarily unrelated persons, sharing costs and chores as needed.[28] Although these practices often make headlines—particularly if they necessitate a challenge to zoning laws or a redefinition of *family* in areas zoned for kinship residences only—we must remember that such multiperson households as boarding houses were once typical of American life, and often provided a necessary income for widowed or separated women. Life-style change frequently occurs within a framework or along a continuum which shows new adaptations of old practices rather than totally new initiatives.

One change which, though by no means new, is certainly newly visible and newly acknowledged, is the practice of cohabitation, both heterosexual and homosexual. Because of the relative openness of American society today—and because heterosexual cohabitation is increasingly unlikely to produce unwanted pregnancy—both these life-styles are acknowledged and often supported by older persons as well as by the young.

Obviously, homosexuality is not a new phenomenon. Estimates are that about one-tenth of our population is homosexual in orientation. We cannot know whether our greater frankness about homosexuality is increasing the percentage of avowed homosexuals or merely their numbers. Certainly many myths about homosexuals are yielding to greater understanding. Among lesbian couples there are many women with children, and their children reflect a very new life-style. These households challenge many common psychiatric assumptions about child development, and raise issues which are coming increasingly into legal and public attention. In many states, homosexual practices, even between consenting adults, are a crime, and lesbians and gay men are still subject to sporadic violence, frequent discrimination, and attacks on their civil rights. There is as yet no legal norm about child custody or care; thus lesbianism is a lifestyle fraught with dangers. Those who publicly acknowledge it show a considerable degree of courage.

Whether it is true that women, with their customary reliance on intense and open friendships with other women, live, as some have asserted, along a lesbian continuum, it is certainly true that women habitually share their concerns with other women, finding a response that they often find no where else. Lesbian women challenge customary assumptions about what women need to be happy and fulfilled, and their presence helps us critique values we often accept without examination. To persons accustomed to living under patriarchy, the presence of women who resist that pressure in the most intimate areas of their lives can help us all examine our own needs and lives honestly. Certainly women need to make common cause with all those who have felt oppression and denial of rights because of the personalities and bodies into which they were born.

With regard to heterosexual cohabitation, open acknowledgment of the life-style is again so recent that assessments are difficult. The once-hoped-for result that premarital cohabitation would lead to better marriages does not appear to have occurred; chances for success in marriages that follow cohabitation and those that do not appear about equal. Disturbingly, violence appears to be somewhat more common among cohabiting couples than among those who are married,[29] and most of these households, far from offering a radical challenge to prevailing sex-role stereotypes, seem to be traditional in their allocation of chores. Heterosexual cohabitation, at least at present, appears to be largely a comfortable housekeeping/sexual arrangement, free from the legal and property regulations which govern marriage. It is also a precursor of marriage and parenthood for many couples, though not necessarily with one another.

Cohabitation may have failed to challenge marriage and parenthood because it has met with so little social opprobrium. Even older persons—including persons past retirement years—have chosen this life-style, which offers intimacy and companionship without the disruptions of inheritance decisions or loss of retirement income that marriage might bring. Courts are increasingly being called upon to settle for unmarried relationships property questions very like those attendant upon marital dissolutions. We should remember that English law has long provided for the existence of "common law" marriages, which appear in many respects to be precursors of the modern practice. Once again a "new" life-style has some very traditional components.

Both cohabitation and sexual activity without marriage are, for women of child-bearing years, life-styles made possible by the existence of birth control and abortion. What is surprising is the degree to which these practices have received social acceptance. Many parents undoubtedly wonder whether the fact that their children often have, over a lifetime, many more sexual partners than they themselves have had will make for greater happiness; many fear the widely reported upsurge in precancerous conditions (especially in women) and venereal disease; many also undoubtedly feel a twinge of regret that the sexual revolution came in their own middle years, rather than in their youth. But widespread parental acceptance—or perhaps resignation—seems to suggest that what passed previously for sexual morality was often a concern about extramarital or premarital pregnancy. Thoughtful persons and religious groups, seeing the line between marriage and cohabitation being blurred, need to ponder what in fact the difference is, in the way of social acceptability, personal commitment, or ethical and legal implications.

Unfortunately, one age group of women often reflects the changed sexual mores of our times without displaying the effects of reliable contraception. The average girl now becomes sexually active at the age of sixteen; 1,100,000 teenage girls become pregnant each year, and about 600,000 of them give birth. Girls under fifteen and women over thirty-five are the only age groups of American women among whom the birth rate is rising.

Resort to abortion for pregnant teenagers is most common for the middle class,[30] which may retain a marked sense of stigma about premarital pregnancy. More likely, the middle class realizes that girls have other options open than early motherhood. Present restrictions on abortion fall most heavily upon the poor, and girls who have and keep their babies run a great risk that they will never complete high school, never hold a good job, never live above the poverty line. Their babies are at risk for premature birth, low birth weight, and child abuse or neglect as they grow up in the care of mothers who are themselves children. Even when society, however grudgingly, steps in to assist these unmarried mothers and their children, we see vividly the feminization of poverty, bearing out a governmental prediction that, by the year 2000, the poor of America will consist almost entirely of elderly women and single-parent women and their children.[31] There appears to be no change in that prediction on the horizon.

We should note in conclusion the life-style changes among older women. As women advance in age toward the seventy-plus years now projected for them, their chances of being alone (usually widowed) increase. Unfortunately, so do their chances of being poor, since a large majority of aging women depend upon property and/or pension accumulated in the husband's name. Women are more likely to end their lives alone or in nursing homes than are men, and for many their lot is a lonely and undignified decline into sickness and death. Still, many older women work, travel, or become socially active, and groups like the Gray Panthers and the Older Women's Legal and Educational Fund keep the needs of older women visible. The female leadership of these groups provides role models that give courage and inspiration. The issue of aging from the woman's perspective should be on the agenda of all political parties. Young women must make aging a primary concern,[32] even though their own relationship to the world of work promises some change in the prospects before them.

WOMEN AND WORK

Whether young or old, modern women find more and more areas of life open. The world of paid labor offers satisfactions and challenges heretofore known primarily by men; consequently, women have entered the work force at a rate of over a million women a year for the past decade. The effects of this experience on their lives and their sense of self can be nothing but profound.

At present over forty-million women are in the paid labor force; almost half of all mothers with children under six were working in 1981, as were nearly two-thirds of all women with children under seventeen.[33] Paul Glick's hope—that pressure on both partners in a marriage to work outside the home would lessen—was apparently based on the assumption that sex role change would free men to become nurturers, as it was freeing women to become breadwinners. But economic and psychological reality has doomed that expectation; most men do not nurture, and most women work out of economic need. Whatever their motivation, the question for most women has now become how to combine marriage and motherhood with the other opportunities now open.

Working outside the home is not the new phenomenon for black women that it is for white, becuse many black women have combined work and childrearing since the time of slavery. But the record number of women of all races in the paid labor force is a new and positive development, paralleling the record number of women now returning to education. These women model new roles for their daughters and granddaughters which will have long-lasting effect.

Because of their new commitment to work outside the home, women press for the very adaptations in the workplace that Glick noted. Slowly we are implementing flextime, on-site child-care or even personal days off for the care of a sick child. Some companies are beginning to explore alternative job benefits, such as payments for childcare in lieu of medical policies that duplicate benefits provided by the other spouse; others are beginning to offer natal leave to men and women. Increasingly we hear of men who refuse geographical moves once considered necessary for professional advancement, often because wives have jobs and families have roots that they wish to keep. These changes come far too slowly, however, and far too rarely; finding adequate childcare is still the working mother's most serious problem.[34] It is a measure of the sexism of our society that neither fathers nor government (the fathers writ large) show equal concern.

Within the home many couples are beginning, probably more as a pragmatic concession to reality than as an articulated matter of philosophy, to assign roles and chores according to convenience, ability, or necessity rather than according to old stereotypes. Two-paycheck marriages, now over half of the total, demand the ability to build household tasks around two time schedules. Some couples have arranged chores and finances through premarital agreements, written or verbal. Still, major difficulties remain, especially for working wives and mothers. Many women who work outside the home spend fewer hours in housework than their homemaker sisters, but receive very little assistance from their husbands.[35] Adding a paid job to an unpaid one makes overload severe for millions of women.

Adding motherhood to a career or job is equally difficult. The effects of taking time out in one's midtwenties can be devastating. This is the period during which female competitors—and most men—are achieving competence and entering into promotion tracks. There is financial loss in motherhood as well: the present estimate is that raising a child from birth to age eighteen will cost the parents an average of $135,000.[36]

Entry into the world of paid labor is possible for most women and essential for many. Payment for work done constitutes an important validation of self that men have known for many years, and that women are coming increasingly to value and expect. For wives and mothers, access to economic regard may enhance their authority within the home; for unmarried women economic self-sufficiency may mean that marriage is not the only route to security or status; for all women participation in the world of paid labor may develop the increased sense of their own value on which all hope for effective change must ultimately depend.

CONCLUSION AND THEOLOGICAL REFLECTIONS

All changes in modern women's lives—changes resulting primarily from their new access to economic rewards and reproductive control—have occurred within the framework of predominantly patriarchal institutions and attitudes. The paradox of family life for women, both now and in the past, has been that both marriage and motherhood have enhanced their vulnerability and dependence, placing them at a profound disadvantage in all aspects of their lives. Until women achieve the transformed sense of self which will enable them to claim from the men with whom they live, for whom they work, and by whom they are governed the legal, psychological, and economic equality that ought to be theirs, they will not achieve the liberation many seek. Women need the insight and courage to declare that the inequalities which they experience in marriage and family are paralleled and mutually reinforced by the economic inequalities of the larger society.[37]

For the vast majority of women, marriage and family are still virtually inevitable life-styles. No thoughtful person would deny the value of either, even in their present state. As Jessie Bernard concluded, both in her original *The Future of Marriage* and its recent revision,

Marriage is the best of human statuses and the worst, and it will continue to be so. And that is why, though its future in some form or another is as assured as anything can be, this future is as equivocal as its past. The demands that men and women make on marriage will never be fully met; they cannot be. And these demands will rise rather than decline as new standards—rightfully—go up. Men and women will continue to disappoint as well as delight one another, regardless of the form of their commitments to one another, or the living style they adopt. . . .

And so now to the first order of business. To upgrade the wife's marriage . . .[38]

To begin that process of upgrading, we need to focus honestly on the present state of women's lives.

That state shows both change and reevaluation. Women are clearly choosing paid work, postponing or rejecting marriage, having fewer children or none at all. In addition, both men and women are challenging the traditional meaning of *family*. Few would deny that the word refers to those related by blood, marriage, or adoption, but many now use the term to describe virtually any life-style, from singleness to communal living. To use the word in such contradictory senses testifies to its power, its ability to suggest the safe haven that family, often more as an ideal than a reality, is supposed to give.

It remains to be seen whether a term stretched in so many directions may not lose its meaning altogether. What is to be feared is that this usage will obscure the reasons for our new lifestyles, reasons often resulting from a justified critique of traditional family life. This expanded usage may indicate a sentimental unwillingness to face reality, so that the "magic word" provides a protective coloration behind which necessary change and challenge may pass unnoticed. We need the courage to be realistic about family experience, its failures as well as its successes, particularly as both affect women. Using the word for deeply different relationships denies both their distinctiveness and the richly paradoxical and therefore fully human realities of family experience.

Upon what basis can a realistic assessment of modern lifestyles proceed, particularly for those of the Judeo-Christian tradition? As heirs to that heritage, we find its teachings a most ambivalent guide. How do the Bible's explicit or tacit assumptions about women's lives help us, grounded as they are in a world so different from our own? How do they apply to the modern world of romantic love, easy marital dissolution, increased longevity (with its consequent stress on relationships), and the almost universal expectation of sexual happiness? How do biblical statements about homosexuality apply to lesbians?

Does the Bible evidence *any* awareness of the actualities of female sexuality?

To seek answers to these questions in our tradition is to be overwhelmed anew by its concentration on male consciousness, male authorship, and male relationships to God. Women worship in religions created out of a male experience, a fact verified by our faith's language, assumptions, and metaphors for God: there is in the Christian tradition no imagery which elevates mother and daughter in ways comparable to its exaltation of Father and Son.

Many of us look hopefully to the life and practice of Jesus, finding in his attitudes toward women a prefiguring of the liberation we seek. Yet we must admit that our reading of his life—of his revelations to the woman at the well, his words to Mary and Martha, his use of women as witnesses, and all the other passages pored over by feminists—was for centuries unnoticed by serious scholarship. It is hard not to wonder whether our new certainties are not at least in part our new creation, born out of our deepfelt need.

But we must believe that the truth will in fact liberate, not only women but also the men with whom in one way or another we all share our lives. We must speak the truth, saying that women have borne a disproportionately heavy share of human suffering, being subject both to the inevitable sorrows of human life and to the particular trials of their sex as well. If men have periodically faced death and suffering in warfare, women have faced them daily in wanted or unwanted pregnancies; they have faced war in the death of the sons that they and other women suffered to bring to birth, and in the rape of themselves and their daughters by exultant warriors. If men have experienced economic exploitation despite hard labor, women have shared both with them, and have seen their own labor devalued below that of men the world over.

Surely if we speak the truth about women's reality—even in a society as privileged as our own—we can awaken both our co-religionists and secular society. To both we must point out the truth of women's subordination and denigration throughout history. At the same time, we must demonstrate that women have experience and wisdom to contribute to our religious and cultural traditions, and that both will be enriched by inclusiveness just as certainly as both have been impoverished by exclusion.

We must affirm the truth and the validity of our special experience, believing that here God's work is truly our own, and that our struggle to give full value to the lives of women, whatever their class or race, their sexual orientation, their age or life-style, is fully in accord with the biblical themes of justice, mercy, and liberation. It is in these great themes that we find the basis from which to reform our faith by our faith.

That reformation depends upon a sense of acceptance and community, a willingness to say with Adrienne Rich in her great poem "From an Old House in America," "Any woman's death diminishes me."[39] To know that truth is to affirm the goodness of God's creation in all its fullness, and to demonstrate that we have moved beyond our culture and our tradition, proclaiming women everywhere as worthy reflections of the divine image. The present moment affords the opportunity to make that affirmation. To seize this creative moment demands courage and faithfulness, both in those who speak and in those who listen. And we must endeavor, despite our anger and our hurt, to speak that truth in love.

6. Liberating Work

CLARE B. FISCHER[1]

Descend into the hell of memory. Love-stricken forever—keep humanity from every crime.[2]

The German phrase *Arbeit macht frei* (work liberates) haunts my thoughts about work, especially as it concerns women's life experience. The phrase possesses an ambiguity, promoting a hopeful vision in the context of a brutalizing reality. For the words, contrary to their message, appeared as a cruel invitation—an inscription upon the main gateway of Auschwitz. To the captive laborer struggling for survival within that infamous camp, the phrase could only mean liberation from a relentless round of harsh effort.

Historical interpretation of work reflects both the promise of the phrase and the grinding abuse of humans in the daily activity of gaining a livelihood. The ancient Greeks disdained labor as freedom's antithesis—a matter of necessity that set apart the population of producers from those concerned with the affairs of polity. But this view has not prevailed in Western history, and today there are positive and negative voices mixed in the chorus of work analysts. Those who offer an optimistic perspective of work's meaning understand the activity as a beneficially transformative one, which assures dignity to the producer. In this view of work as the freeing of potential individual capacity, identity, community, and spiritual knowledge are unified through

Clare Benedicks Fischer is the Aurelia Henry Reinhardt Professor of Religion and Culture at Starr King School for Religious Leadership in Berkeley, California. In addition to instructing classes in world religions and feminist theology, she currently serves as the convenor of the Graduate Theological Union's (Berkeley) area specialty in the history and phenomenology of religions. She is active in community groups working against family violence, serving on the boards of an antidomestic violence coalition and an anti-incest group.

engagement of the mind, hand, and soul. Baum's recent commentary on work provides an excellent example of this positive way of approaching the subject.[3]

The phrase "work liberates" has a grim side when seen in the light of generations of laborers who have relentlessly performed in debilitating settings in order to survive. Here the sense of liberation is one that the worker holds is being *free from* onerous tasks, the arbitrary will of supervisors, the marginality of wage and benefit. Transformation takes on a negative meaning, a veritable reversal of the more optimistic perspective of those who project dignity and social construction for the worker. Rather, labor extracts effort that diminishes the self—severing the mind from the body, violating the standards of health and well-being of the individual, fragmenting accomplishment and distancing one laborer from another. From the perspective of labor, liberation is a goal that minimizes pain, boredom, exploitation and expands opportunity for as much free time as can be negotiated.

Although there are social commentaries that praise the progress of economic activity in this century, the harshness of production and the stress of service work persists. Generally described under the rubric of rationalized labor (or "Taylorism"), this structuring of the work experience intensifies the pressure upon the producer to meet quotas and to eliminate activities that are inefficient. Historically this organization of work was associated with industrial assembly lines, but in recent decades it has spread to white-collar work and the computer-electronics industry.[4] Subordination of workers' purposes to industrial demands for high output serve to elevate the values of dexterity, docility, and indifference. Despite the claims of industrial human relations and technological innovation, managers and engineers have not substantially increased job satisfaction nor have they reduced the alienation which contributes to individual and social illness. The "quality of working life" movement does not penetrate the global assembly line of the offices that employ thousands of women in postindustrial and Third World nations.

A third reading of the German phrase yields another interpretation of liberating work—this, perhaps, the most ironic. Women's work has been historically buried under definitions and analyses that devalue and deny effort except as it contributes to family life.[5] Even in this domestic understanding, the persistent activity of women has been trivialized and perceived as a non-work, a mere enactment of anatomical destiny. Amitra Pritram, the Indian poet, expresses the violence of this exclusion:

> "My wife does not work."
> But then,
> Who bears the tiller, the toiler that the world
> goes on?
> Who does the cooking, the cleaning, the washing? . . .
> Whose work provides the daily energy for the man
> to earn a wage, for the children to go to school?
> Whose labor, unseen, unheard, unpaid, underpaid,
> unrecognized?[6]

The assumption of nonproductivity attached to the work of women fosters an ideology of gender difference that distorts the notion of freedom. The hidden reality of everyday economic activity is simply free from public account but is certainly experienced by the laborer and those who benefit from the effort.

Study of women's work from a number of disciplinary perspectives and theoretical orientations indicates that the devaluation of both domestic and marketplace activity lies in cultural bias.[7] Feminist theology has identified some of the sources that proliferate an ideology of woman's social subordination and her dismissal as "other." This effort has insisted upon the unveiling of stereotype and false consciousness that conceal woman's presence as active, intelligent, co-creator. Carter Heyward's recent criticism of the distancing, abstract theology that separates humans from one another and from divinity is particularly useful for a feminist theology of work.[8] Her embrace of concrete relationship that is intimate and immediate as the ground of social justice provides a point of departure for my own analysis.

It may be that woman's work as a taken-for-granted activity has something to do with interpretive schemes that overlook the obvious. Yves Simon commented that work's meaning is "hidden in the mystery of familiarity," an observation that hints at an underpinning of cultural denial.[9] Clearly, the interior labors of women (in homes, in sweatshops, in other isolated spaces) have less visibility than those performed by men in public places.

Arendt's well-known separation of labor and work supports this understanding, describing the accomplishments of *animal laborans* (the laboring human-animal) as necessary but without esteem.[10] Woman's repetitive labors in the production of goods and services that are consumed immediately and therefore unenduring are perceived in Arendt's terms as lacking the vitality of world-building (as in the work of the *homo faber*).

The forms of violence generated in the workplace that disable and devalue the worker are many; so, too, the humiliations emerging from nonwork. Much has been written in the past twenty years about alienation and the diminution of the human person in the performance of so ordinary an activity as work.[11] Camus's observation that unemployment damages but "when work is soulless, life stifles and dies" continues to have meaning today. In the remarkable testimonies of workers assembled by Studs Terkel, a veritable chorus of the dis-spirited resonates, reminding the reader that men and women share a common reality.[12] Terkel introduces this collection of interviews with the statement that a book about work is of necessity a book about violence exacted against mind, body, and spirit. Nora Watson, an interviewee, attests to this, remarking that "jobs are not big enough for people." The perception of marginality, the elusiveness of purpose beyond the doing of a job, has perilous consequences for individuals and for the social order.

Women have entered the world's paid labor force in dramatic numbers, and their participation invites a novel discussion of work's meaning as an entitlement for all. The editor of a UNESCO study on work writes of the paradoxical turns in current employment practices and work ideals, indicating the growing distance between principle and practice.[13] He suggests that the international vision of "full employment" as stated in the *Universal Declaration of Human Rights* has become a dimmer possibility in view of automation, job displacement, industrial shifts. Yet women in advanced and so-called developing economies have secured wage work and contributed to the emergence of a worldwide "feminization of labor."

But the shifts in labor force participation have not dispelled the pervasive ideology of woman as "reproducer" rather than "producer." The omission of rural Third World women's work from the calculations of international estimates of "production boundaries" reveals this exclusionary practice vividly.[14] Although 50 percent of the Third World's food is produced by three million women, according to International Labor Organization statistics, fetching, hauling (water and fuel), digging, harvesting, storing activity remain invisible labor. Not only is this manual effort left out of reports but women's needs and requirements for this activity fail to be included in the deliberations of development specialists. Fiscal assistance, technological improvements, and other strategies that would have radically beneficial consequences for the agriculturally productive woman are not forthcoming.[15] Moreover, women in almost every part of the world share in being exempted from accounts of work with respect to a variety of their domestic chores (such as caring for children, the sick, the elderly, as well as maintaining the home).

The illusion thrives that woman's "vocation" is materially distinguishable from the consequences of man's productive activity. It not only surfaces in the denial of international economics but is communicated by other prominent international figures. In the recent papal encyclical addressed to the subject of work (*Laborem exercens*), Pope John Paul II differentiates the work of men and women, particularly in regard to the struggle for liberation from oppressive practices in the workplace.[16] Despite the document's impressive identification of human work with dignity, with the positive construction of world history, the lens narrows as it focuses upon woman's primary destiny as wife and mother. One critic of the encyclical expresses anxiety over the prestigious character of a document that conveys such a cultural blindness toward women. In a sense, the progressive tone proves to be all the more damning to women who secure livelihood along the international assembly line.[17] This criticism is joined by Baum who remarks that the omission of women from the discussion of institutional injustice and the struggle for liberation is regrettable.[18]

Despite the obstinancy of images and myths that diminish the role of women in material history, factual realities have begun to press upon and undermine prejudice. The traditional pattern of relegating woman's activity to a secondary or supportive place is no longer justified with the revelation of census data that indicates a dramatic rise in the woman "breadwinner." Family life and the expectations of women and men are being shaped by demographic changes that suggest a permanent modification of the world's labor force. The implications of this work-population revolution are many—some good, some bad— revealing again the complex and ambiguous character of human work. I identify six trends that seem to be most important for the American worker and warn that each represents only a surface statement about worklife that reaches to all institutions and values. They are:

1. the dramatic rise in participation—double the number of paid women in the workforce since 1950 (approximately 45 million);
2. the growth in number of married women in the workforce—five times the participation since 1940 (approximately 24 million women);
3. the continuing difference in men's work and women's earnings—women make approximately fifty-nine cents for every dollar earned by men (in 1979, the median annual earnings of full-time women workers was almost $7,000 less);
4. in the past twenty years the number of female-headed households (with children under eighteen years) has doubled (66 percent of these women were in the labor force in 1979);
5. the unemployment rate for minority women is greater than other groups according to 1979 figures (approximately 12.3 percent);
6. the female labor force is clustered (some 80 percent) in low-paying occupational categories (clerical, sales, service, factory).[19]

Analysis of these trends would dislodge a number of related issues for the working woman, including discrimination in unions and in nontraditional work, sexual harassment on the job, and occupational hazards affecting reproductive health.

These developments in the labor force provide convincing evidence of the ambiguity of work, with movement (rapid entry of women in the paid sector) and the status quo (ghettoization and differential wage) simultaneously giving shape to the American economy. The dramatic increase in employed women is a world-wide phenomenon with some 35 percent of women active in the global workforce (in 1975); many participate in "labor-intensive manufacturing plants that depend on low-paid female labor."[20]

The promise of economic autonomy is compounded by an increase—not a slackening—of responsibility. Married and single working mothers return to their homes in every part of the globe after a full day of paid labor only to resume the chores that they have traditionally performed: cooking, cleaning, repairing of clothes, care for the children. Petchesky observes, "Working in production and reproducing are increasingly simultaneous, superimposed occupations for women—held in an uneasy tension, misleadingly called the 'double day,' because there is never any neat division where one job begins and the other ends."[21]

Women throughout the world participate in the movement toward the "feminization of poverty," which clearly demonstrates an inextricable connection of family and work. A rapid increase in female responsibility for subsistence has emerged, in part, because of breakdown in the traditional family structure. In the United States in 1979, women constituted three-fourths of the population classified as impoverished, and of that number, blacks, Hispanics, and the elderly represented a substantial percentage of the poor. In Third World countries, women are also surviving below standards of decent nutrition, health, housing. Many have been left behind in villages that are virtually abandoned by male adults and single young women who migrate to cities in search of employment. This nomadic pattern is occurring wherever dependable means of livelihood have disappeared—in modernizing economies of the Third World, in post-industrial nations that have witnessed plant closures and job displacement in ever-growing numbers.

I have identified three approaches that underpin the distortion in attitude and practice regarding woman's work. Each represents an ideological structure that generates and sustains difference and hierarchy in the workworld. Each possesses a nuanced value-orientation that promotes and legitimates the devaluation of and discrimination against women in their daily activity of earning a wage, of securing an adequate environment for the family. All three structures are intertwined in the funda-mental assumption about the *naturalness* of differentiated labor according to gender.

The division of labor according to sexual identity is the most persistent structure, with its separation of woman as biologically limited and man as world-builder. In this approach, body and mind are first separated according to gender and then perceived as rightfully reconciled in the balanced and distinctive effort of the two sexes.

Similarly, a second division of work according to location or space assumes the symbolic and real division and unification of the sexes—woman as wife/mother in the home, man as bread-winner in the marketplace. Curiously, in this version of division of labor, virtue is reversed. Woman emerges in the industrial world as the incarnation of protective goodness, securing for her family a veritable retreat from the polluting realities of the city.

A third motif, perhaps the most pernicious for women, arises, which assumes the distinctive personality of gender and segre-gates occupational opportunity accordingly. In this division of labor according to feminine and masculine attributes, women are stereotyped as "helpmates" and believed to be particularly suited for the work of assisting, supporting, tending—all efforts that demand patience and a pleasing presence.

The following review of these ideological patterns is prelimi-nary but, one hopes, suggestive of the resilience of prejudice against woman's productive activity. I have infused a feminist perspective into the material, indicating that sexism, classism and racial/ethnic oppression are fundamentally connected. Moreover, the disclosure of the negative (as false consciousness) is offered as a first step, a necessary one, toward the rejection of debilitating attitudes and the resistance against discriminatory practice. Although there is ample basis for pessimism in the face of obstinate devaluation of woman's work, I echo here Rosemary Radford Ruether's caveat that we embrace "hope in the midst of defeat."

Within the discussion of each of the divisive ideologies I have included a visionary corrective, inviting the reader to appreciate the inspiration of certain women who have said "no" to oppres-sion. Simone Weil's search for reform in the industrial workrooms of France represents one expression of a positive transformation of woman's labor. Charlotte Perkins Gilman offers a utopian image of the collaborative home that frees woman for works that contribute to a less privatized environment. Carolina Maria deJesus' endurance in the impoverished life of a shantytown teaches us how vocation can be guarded from the terrors of daily survival. Finally, the figure of Gertie Nevels appears as, for me, the paradigmatic worker who will prevail despite the tyranny of home and worklife through her solidarity with other women. Gertie is a literary creation in Harriet Arnow's classic study of American work history, *The Dollmaker*.

THE SEXUAL DIVISION OF LABOR

... It is tempting to argue that the sexual division of labor is patterned by the biological and reproductive differences between men and women.[22]

The question of origins is generally attached to the discussion of the sexual division of labor and certainly gives rise to the fixity of man-woman work role. Anthropologists have contributed substantially to the knowledge of diversity in work practices and invite an appreciation of its complex structures and enactments among the peoples of the earth. However, much of an earlier ethnography has recently come under scrutiny by feminist anthropologists because the character of field work and the organizing assumptions are judged to be androcentric.[23] Essentially, the consequence of a nonseeing or biased field analysis of gender-defined work roles appears to be the replication of a Western stereotypical understanding of division.

The prevailing view of anthropology has been one that mirrors the biblical narrative of the Fall. In the Genesis account, transgression brings about division. As a consequence of disobedience, the primal couple are expelled from the idyllic setting of the garden where work was both painless and undifferentiated. But with the departure from Eden, another rupture occurs, separating humans from paradise and dividing man and woman in their respective works/destinies. Eve becomes the first "reproducer" and Adam the first "producer." This mythic account has informed centuries of discussion about a divinely ordained purpose that differentiates the two sexes.

The severing of human work into the responsibility for continuation of the species (woman's destiny) and the responsibility for food acquisition and cultural creation (man's work) is not a simple distinction in function. It represents the division of human life as thinking and doing, as mindful and body-determined. Woman becomes associated with body and man with the establishment of the social order, the manufacture of artifacts, the communication of ideas and normative standards.

It is precisely this type of reductionism that Ortner's now classic essay sought to reflect.[24] Arguing against "genetic determinism" of the stronger male, or a more naturally disposed gender for leadership, Ortner identifies the conflation of man with culture, woman with nature as the basis of a ubiquitous subordination of the latter. She explains that this distinction is about "conceptual categories" that rank the activities of the two sexes according to proximity to the natural. Three facets of woman's activity justify a belief in "closer" association to nature: reproduction, lactation, and the socialization of young children. Ortner concludes that it is not this obviously critical life-generating, supporting activity that is devalued but, rather, that nature is perceived as less than, or is transcended by, culture. Men, conversely, are perceived as active in the affairs of the community and thereby free from diminution in the lower status of nature-workers.

Although Ortner's conclusion points to the mediational position of women between nature (as reproducers) and culture (as socializers of the young), her elaboration of a culture-transcending-nature theory promotes understanding of a stratified work force based upon sexual difference. Another scholar has joined Ortner in her caution with respect to biological reductionism and its assumption of a rigid separation in work role. Sanday suggests in her review of three patterns, that separation between men and women in the cultures of the world is more pervasive than not. She observes that the distinction between collaborative and competitive styles of livelihood are not a matter of biological given but of cultural selectivity. "It is not that women cannot hunt or go to war," Sanday writes, but "that motherhood, gentleness, and forgiveness do not mix well with predation, toughness, and warlikeness."[25] Her analysis reflects the findings of investigators who have turned attention to the ethological data about primate sexual differentiation in order to better grasp the notion of separate disposition and activity.

Current inquiry into the meaning of dominance and status in primal groups has reopened the discussion of gathering/hunting as distinctive modes of survival and their respective gender shape.[26] Some research has shown that women have, indeed, participated in small hunting activities but that men rarely participate in food preparation and storage work. Earlier assumptions about woman's biological limitations (maternity and fatigue in physical activity) have begun to be eroded in the assessment of distances traversed in foraging, mobility with children, and the centrality of gathering in the maintenance of life. While higher status does not seem to be accorded women for their food-sharing, cooperative activity, it has been suggested in these recent studies that status and the asymmetry of work roles is a function of symbolic systems and not biological capacity.

The variation in sexual division of roles disproves any simple correlation of gender with productive activity. Not only are there cultural groups which are egalitarian, separating tasks according to gender but without hierarchy (a genuine reciprocity of work), there are variations on the theme of difference and ranked or preferred labors. There is little evidence that there had been an original equality in horticulture or in earlier foraging culture, and there is every certainty that traditional culture participates in history and has felt the long arm of colonialism with respect to gender role. What can be concluded is that an association of dominance over nature with the male has its basis in the symbolic orientations of both primal and biblical people, and that such dominance assumes a superiority of those who control nature. MacCormack indicates the consequences of an opposition between human dominion and nature.

When women are defined as "natural" a high prestige of even moral "goodness" is attached to men's domination over women, analogous to the "goodness" of human domination of natural energy resources or the libidinal energy of individuals.[27]

Susan Griffin's elaboration of the historical dominion of men over the "natural," including animals and women, persuasively indicates the ill-effects of this separation and arrogance for humanity.[28]

One implication of the sexual division of labor as an ideology of superiority and subordination is the emergence of a gender specific assembly line created by the postindustrial multinational. Two dimensions of this "feminization of global industry" emerge: the exportation of exploitation and the more current importation of cheap labor in the semiconductor industry. In Southeast Asia, most notably Malaysia and Indonesia, single women have been recruited in large numbers to labor in electronic, textile, and garment industries. Personnel literature, according to Grossman's study of this feminized production,[29] entices the inexperienced Asian female to seek employment with promises of a good income, recreational benefits, and a modern lifestyle. What the female recruit does not enjoy, however, is a good wage, healthful surroundings, a decent workpace, and the security of her employment. Her alleged feminine attributes are perceived as attractive: "variously described as 'cheap,' 'docile,' 'nimbled-fingered,' and 'well-fit by nature for monotonous work.'"[30] It is estimated that 85 percent of Third World workers are women and that they are preferred precisely because they are economically vulnerable. Moreover, some personnel material indicates that the traditional activity of these women—sewing, weaving—is particularly suited for the type of assembly effort required in the semiconductor industry.

Grossman reports that resistance has begun to surface among these women in the form of protests, sit-ins, and slow-downs. She adds that one promising activity involves tours of women from one country to another in quest of solidarity. Philippine women, for example, visited the assembly rooms of Hong Kong in an effort to forge links in the movement for better working conditions.

Research about California's "Silicon Valley," the site of semiconductor production in the United States, reveals the integrated character of the global factory system.[31] In the past decade, this industry has benefited from the labors of women here and abroad who are obliged (without benefit of unionization) to accept low wages and marginal, unhealthy work conditions. Recruitment policy in the United States is not dissimilar from that promotional activity conducted in Southeast Asia, relying upon feminine stereotypes and assurances of a better life.[32] New employees are told that assembly work is as easy as "following a recipe."

The widening gap between the de-skilled woman worker and the expert engineer in earnings, satisfaction, and mobility is dramatic. Mind and body are virtually severed, the specialist exercising "hi-tech" know-how while the laborer suspends thought and imagination during work hours. It is, indeed, ironic that the industry most advanced in the communications sector profits from the dexterity and desperation of immigrant women.

When Simone Weil entered the factory system of France fifty years ago, industrial exploitation was particularly central in the discussion of proleterian revolution. Weil sought to discover, through firsthand observation and work, whether such grueling labor would inspire resistance and worker solidarity.[33] Her findings, based upon immediate and intimate daily engagement with arbitrary foremen, broken and hazardous machinery, disheartened workers, provided little solace for labor union organizers and Marxist activists. She experienced a brutality to her soul that she perceived as even more devastating for the workers (principally women and migrants from Algeria)—a diminution and humiliation that developed apathy rather than rage.

Weil's alarm at the demeaning practices of a rationalized labor system did not cease with her yearlong factory experience. She wrote and spoke publicly condemning work speedups, the injustices of piece-rate wage, the isolation and joylessness of activity. "In such a situation," she reiterated in her criticism, "the subordinate is almost like an inert object used as a tool by the intelligence of another."[34] But she did not avoid constructive appeals to her audience of factory managers and union leaders. She presented a program that was, then, perceived as idealistic and unworkable. Today, many of her reform suggestions emerge in the discussion of "democratic worker participation."

The gist of her vision for the humanization of industrial workrooms (which assumed the improbability of worker revolution and the transformation of economic ideology) went to the core of "de-skilling" strategies still advanced by management. She called for the adequate orientation of every worker, including tours of the entire production process and explanation of the specialization and division of tasks. This would inform every participant along the production circuit, alleviating some sense of distance between individual and activity. In addition, each expert would make appearances in the workroom, provide information, and listen to the on-line laborer. With such an exchange of knowledge (theoretical and practical), Weil hoped that respect and understanding would emerge—permitting the arrogance of mind-workers to absorb the intelligent concerns of the production laborer.

Variation in task was an important reform, as was the demand for adequate ventilation, reduction of noise, decent recreational spaces, and the replacement of automatic machinery for humans where assembly effort was totally repetitious. When "things play the role of men (*sic*), men the role of things," the scale of production and its apparatus must be changed for the benefit of workers. Weil's vision also assumed the autonomy of work units and the creation of programs that would stimulate independent and social accomplishment (including worker education). Her plan insisted upon a decent standard of income for the job performed but resisted settling for a monetary interpretation of what needed to be done to rectify the demeaning circumstance of labor.[35]

The hopes of that French academic, who could not be content with abstract criticism of capitalism and was propelled into the oppressive conditions of the workroom, continue to be relevant in today's world of international labor. In Weil's refusal to ignore the deep issues of worker alienation, the pain of sacrificing human values and expectations in order to earn a livelihood, Weil refused division. Her desire to "re-member" the laborer embraced the whole person as mind/body, the person as community based, and the person whose destiny required a lively spirit.[36] She did not relent in her exposure of labor conditions, nor did she abandon her effort to reeducate managers and corporate executives about the centrality of humane work for modern civilization. She incarnated Heyward's relational actor (p. 119) who works for social justice in an intimate and immediate way.

THE SEPARATION OF SPHERES: HOME AND WORK

As long as private lives and public institutions are arranged around the assumption that the home is a female province, women's opportunities for achievement in other domains will be limited.[37]

Historians indicate that the separation of work and home as we know it in the twentieth century accompanied the rise of industrialization at the beginning of the last century.[38] Women's work in the home (the making of clothing, soap, and so on) was transformed into factory work that depended principally upon male labor. Less than 3 percent of Massachusetts's female population was employed in that state's textile mills in 1832. Almost all were single and left industrial work as soon as they married. In fact, this number did not grow substantially, and in 1900 only 5 percent of the labor force included married women. However, this statistic indicates more than the spread in gender-defined labor. It represents an ideology of separate realms that depended upon the submission of women and an acceptance of life purpose as wife and mother attached to the family hearth.

Women's role was idealized in the "cult of domesticity" that promoted a view of labor force production as necessary but male-occupied. Women who sought paid employment were perceived as "either unfortunate or deliberately perverse." The realities for the former included marginal wages, opportunity in jobs that required laundering, child-tending, and other "domestic" tasks. For those who wished to be economically independent from parents or spouse, the discriminatory practices emerging from an ideology that defined woman as naturally and instinctively destined only for homelife turned many potential women workers back to the family. What the "cult of domesticity" assured was the internalization of values that elevated woman as a pivotal figure in the morality of her immediate relationships as well as those of the nation. A plethora of woman's guidebooks fostered this notion of superiority and provided justification for the homebound woman who need not seek gratification of identity from the "outside" world.

The elements of this ideology that were central to this task were, first, that children required full-time, undivided adult attention; second, that women were specifically endowed to provide this care (and to create the homes that their husbands needed as well); and, finally, that domesticity would shield women from the evil of the outside world and bring them status and power mediated through their families.[39]

Two points about the ideological enticements of domesticity should be made. Both suggest the dominance of the middle class in shaping the hearth-work split. Activists in the first wave of feminism were principally drawn from privileged circumstances and had little understanding of the seductive character of domesticity. Although attention was given by these women to abuses of marriage law, very little was said about the marginalization of the woman in the home or her disability as a dependent upon her spouse's income. The more radical critics (including Susan B. Anthony, Elizabeth Cady Stanton, and Victoria Woodhull) recognized the issue of autonomy but failed to connect the divisive pattern with industrial developments and the role of women as supportive of this economic system.

Moreover, the cult of domesticity—while enacted principally in the privileged homes of the middle class—was shared as an ideal by most women, including the newly arrived immigrant who joined the labor force in order to provide for her family. The neat compartmentalization of tasks, the dialectic of male-worker, female-mother/wife, was generally embraced as a virtuous division which gave every family member a special destiny in the building of a strong nation. This sentiment persisted into the present century, emerging in the second decade as the promise of a "decent family wage" that would allow the man of the home to be totally responsible for bread-winning.[40]

Among feminist scholars interested in the implications for women in new work patterns, many have focused on the meaning of housework in the context of role performance and actual energy output. There is a general agreement among these researchers that the home-work ideology continues to foster disadvantages for women whether independently employed or working exclusively in the confines of the home. A continuing asymmetry in responsibility for the upkeep of the home is reported, which further divides the work of men and women.[41]

Newland suggests that the specialization of housework remains with women, although they have assumed additional work in the paid labor force as well. This activity unites women everywhere who experience a heavy workload in the uncompensated servicing of family.[42] Vanek observes that the purchase of labor-saving devices in the modern home has not substantially lifted the pressure from women in the performance of their housework.[43] On the contrary, the advertising industry has merely increased standards of adequacy and enticed employed and nonemployed women alike to engage in an unending busyness to assure a clean, attractive environment.

In addition to the traditional expenditure of energy in making a home fit for its members, women have also committed themselves to a "home-work" that resembles the cottage industry of an earlier age. Some women, a small number, have discovered talents that can be put to use in securing supplementary income or "free" products (including saleswork in the neighborhood for Avon, Tupperware, and so on). Another group of women, among them illegals from Latin America and Asia, secure piece-rate contracts with garment and microchip contractors to assemble parts at home. Katz and Kleinmetz indicate that this retrograde industrial practice allows companies to elude wage and health standards that have been put into place after decades of labor struggle. While this "home-work" provides income for women who must remain at home with children, it exploits their vulnerability and fosters an invisible class of laborers—racial-ethnic women hidden in the private space of the home.

A dialectical tension emerges between the gender roles of producer and reproducer when grasped in the ordinary experiences of women who labor in the home. Clearly, productive effort that augments the assembly line disrupts any simple assignment of women as nonproductive in the economic affairs of the country. There are other activities that are unpaid which contribute to the vitality of the economy, including volunteer work, which is overwhelmingly conducted by women. Nonprofit organizations, churches, and schools depend upon the gratuitous effort of the volunteer whose work assures the smooth operation of agency and institution.

Nona Glazer's recent study critizes the way work has been

conceptualized as either paid (marketplace) or unpaid (household).[44] In her analysis of retail sales, Glazer reveals the presence of "involuntary unpaid work" that is performed by women as consumers. Her insightful exploration of boundaries between home and market indicates that "self-service" retailing involves work that is unrecognized. Historically, men occupied sales positions but were displaced by the feminization of this occupation; with self-service retailing, the consumer performs the work formerly held by the salesperson, and the industry secures only the paid labor of a de-skilled cashier. Involuntary unpaid labor is distinguished from volunteer effort, being perceived as family-oriented activity.

The labor has the appearance of being privatized, isolated work so characteristic of women's domestic labor . . . the work can be seen as central to the distribution of goods. . . . Here it is not that wages are less than embodied in labor power but that the labor is coerced, enlisted without the consumer being aware of it.[45]

The scope of the "reproductive" role has also been enlarged by current feminist analysis. Recognition of woman's multiple activity in the home is advanced as activity that cannot be distinguished from the more visible efforts of the productive worker. In addition to the biological labor of replenishing the species, two other modes of reproduction are identified in the context of the home. All the "family care" associated with household maintenance is classified as socially reproductive labor that assures labor power; the laborer depends upon woman's work (following nineteenth-century ideological assumptions) for nutrition, recreation, sexual pleasure. Women also reproduce the socio-ideological system in the socialization of their children. This work, classified by Ortner as mediational between nature and culture, is the least privatized in consequence, although it is performed in the private sphere of the home. Each of these reproductive labors has been integrated in a program demanding *wages* for housework. Little agreement exists among feminists about this strategy, but all agree that the cultural myopia towards housework as *real* work must be overcome through education and the dispelling of fallacious dichotomies.

Almost a century ago, one feminist writer rejected the tyranny of dualism and demanded that home and work be reconciled in an egalitarian economy. Charlotte Perkins Gilman's classic study, *Women and Economics,* recognized the danger that women were placed in as economic dependents, and she sought to find a viable strategy that would change the expectations of women and men with respect to their alleged destinies.[46] She attacked the stereotypes of gender-nature and sexual duty, suggesting that the human personality was essentially ungendered.

Gilman's writing career was dedicated to restoring the balance and health of a population obsessed with personality difference based upon gender. She insisted that a better world shaped by reciprocity and cooperation could emerge with the reconstruction of work patterns and the modification of homelife. Perhaps the most challenging of her reforms was the institution of what has come to be called the symmetrical family. Gilman wished to see men in home responsibility and women in the workplace. Hers was not a reversal of role location and performance but an exchange grounded on aptitude and fairness. The isolated household was to be modified by structural changes that would involve communal food-preparation/sharing, and the "sordid shop" was to be reformed for all—male and female. In this vision, Gilman critized selfishness (in production and consumption) and the one-sided selflessness of the woman household worker. She hoped that one day "we shall live in a world of men and women related, working together, as they were meant to do, for the common good of all."

Gilman's work continues to hold a promise for family cooperation that establishes the freedom of women to secure employment in the paid sector and the freedom of men to contribute to the work of the home in substantial ways. These hopes would effectively modify socialization that continues to charge woman with almost absolute responsibility for child care and housework and exempt men from the domestic labors performed by wives and daughters.

THE DIVISION OF ASPIRATION AND OPPORTUNITY

As they demand the opportunity to earn success, to acknowledge ambition, to develop competence, to assume leadership, to acquire power, to try to risk in the ways that men have, women are making a bold statement that they also, like men, are individuals.[47]

The identification of women with the domestic sphere and men with the marketplace has been associated with personality theory or notions of socialization. Exclusionary employment patterns, described as gender "occupational segregation," tap into an ideology of feminine and masculine attributes sometimes equated with "expressive" and "instrumental" values and roles. Men are perceived as better able to work rationally and steadily with undivided commitment to the task. Women, conversely, are stereotyped as immature, timid with respect to job demands, and best suited for work that builds upon learned domestic skill.

The clustering of employed women in fields that utilize alleged feminine dispositions and values has been the subject of a number of studies.[48] Some analysts have traced it to family informal education of gender identity, indicating that girls and boys learn in the earliest years to distinguish themselves with respect to appropriate activity in the home, in school, in the community.[49] Independence and a pattern of "early breakaway" from the restraints of family life seem to be correlated with the learning boys receive; girls, conversely, are inculcated with a compassionate sensibility that invites greater dependence and the deferring of self-interest. "Society," writes Nancy Barrett, "has long encouraged women to accept vicarious satisfactions."[50] She adds that socialization which models the father as authority and the mother as subordinate fosters a view internalized by women that accomplishment belongs to the male. Where women have broken through into executive positions they have discovered difficulty both in the office and at home in being taken seriously, in having their authority respected.

The clustering of occupational roles for women has implications for inequitable earnings and for the arbitrary harassment of women in nontraditional workplaces. Women remain overwhelmingly represented in the clerical-secretarial sector (99 percent), and as dental assistants (98 percent), but recent U.S. Labor Department estimates indicate that women have entered certain nontraditional categories' in striking number.[51] These positions include insurance adjusters, bill collectors, real estate agents and brokers, checkers and production-line assemblers. Despite this trend, the pervasive attitude toward the nontraditional female is best expressed by this woman cable TV installer: "When I applied for the job, they asked me if I was ready to carry heavy equipment. After carrying five children around, it was really easy to say, 'I'm ready.' "[52]

Occupational segregation functions as a dis-incentive for women, either preventing them from horizontal entry into work categories regarded as masculine or obviating mobility within the occupation (vertical segregation). In either case, it prevents women from securing positions that pay well, assure growth, stimulate interest and strong commitment to the work. Although much has been made of the precedent-breaking activities of women during World War II, recent research unveils the mythic character of "Rosie the Riveter," who did not perform novel tasks in any substantial way.[53] Milkman's exposé of the persistence of feminine stereotype on the job during World War II provides ample proof of the resilience of the ideology of womanly aptitude. She explores the domestic translations of job description and the discrepancy in wage accorded to women.

Nursing has been perceived as the exemplary "feminine ghetto." Lewin explains that it is a semiprofession composed of 98 percent women, but, of the small percentage of men in the occupation, a disproportion holds visibly important posts—including supervisorial responsibility.[54] She alleges that the maternal model of nursing conflated with the woman nurse serves to restrict mobility for women. "The close acquaintance of the nurse with the messy private details of illness is not unlike the mother's necessary involvement with infantile body functions." In spite of the low esteem and relative immobility of the female nurse, Lewin believes there is opportunity for women to discover among themselves the strengths and supportive strategies that such a community of workers shares.

Programs of affirmative action have contributed to the breakdown in firmly held bias. Experiences of women on the job convince traditional men and women that alleged gender aptitudes and limitations have little relevance in the daily performance of work. Moreover, the expansion of programs and opportunities for women in vocational training (in crafts and trades) is underway and should begin to erode the clustering pattern that has marked American employment in the past generation.

The courage and vitality of women who have, in fact and in fiction, practiced their vocations can only have beneficial consequences for those who are exploring new ways. The beauty of Carolina Maria deJesus' writing about life in the Brazilian *favela* comes to mind as an exceptional teaching source.[55] In her journal of poverty and the grim survival of the disinherited, deJesus conveys an unwavering belief in herself and the possibility of moving away from the tyranny of shantytown life. She dreams, aspires through her relentless writing, and succeeds. As a matter of veritable accident, her work is discovered and published, and Carolina deJesus secures the recognition and well-being that she had hoped for.

When I write I think I live in a golden castle that shines in the sunlight. . . . I must create this atmosphere of fantasy to forget that I am in a favela.[54]

The extraordinary circumstances of deJesus' vocation are, indeed, a poor model for women struggling to integrate aspiration and opportunity. However, the determination and transcending quality of her effort assure us that empowerment is not available only to the privileged.

Harriet Arnow's remarkable epic novel about the migration of an Appalachian family to Detroit during the Second World War (*The Dollmaker*) provides another glimpse of vocation as struggle and commitment.[57] Perhaps the strongest woman in American literary creation, from the perspective of adaptive skills and unshakable love, is Gertie Nevels. In the development of this fictional woman the reader learns of a dream that cannot be dimmed by all the violence of industrial inequity and family stress. Gertie Nevels brings her woodcarving with her to the slum community of Detroit and continues to work her vocation (as an aesthetic interpreter of human vulnerability, betrayal, survival) in spite of circumstances that would break the spirit of most. But the clear message of her vocation is that isolated activity and talent can never suffice; Gertie manages because she shares in a community that cuts across class and race. At the end of the novel, Gertie's original design is sacrificed—her head representing Christ is chopped into many pieces so that Gertie may "manu-facture" dolls that will provide (in a veritable cottage industry) income for the family. She tells the woodchopper that a single face would not suffice: "There was so many would ha done; they's millions an millions a faces plenty fine enough—fer him."[58] Her neighbors, the community that endures and strug-gles together against humiliation and oppression, are the face of Christ.

CONCLUSION

Liberated work is not an impossible dream. It emerges in every workplace where apathy and fatigue have been transformed into rage and a sense of survival. The historical bias that has kept women from recognition, from self-esteem, from the supports and advantages that productive effort ought to yield to every worker will be dispelled. The words of the Polish survivor of Auschwitz's terror-ridden slave labor pleads with us that we—oppressor/oppressed—discover love through our suffering: "Come awake . . . to an eternity of kindness."[59]

Knowledge, compassion, and direct engagement in change must be joined in that transforming activity. Simone Weil's insis-tence upon disclosure and the distribution of ideas and tech-niques offers one side of the strategy for a radically transformed work. This vision requires a retrieval of history from the ac-counts of powerful figures who have little commitment to mar-ginal persons—women, Third World workers, and so on. Her recognition and passionate condemnation of the transformation of people into things reappears in the scholarship of women studying development policy, reappears in the voices of Third World women who are making strong demands to be represented in all phases of economic planning and implementation. "Only a redefinition of the aim of development process," writes June Nash about Bolivia and the tin-mining industry, "which will put people at the center of planning and reject the exploitation of natural riches for short-run gains will reverse the situation."[60]

The obstinacy that informs Gilman's restructured society where home and workplace are united in cooperative attach-ment resonates in the hopeful visions of feminist activism. There will be a time when woman's exclusive responsibility for family care will be seen as an archaic pattern. There will be a time when the steady focus of Carolina Maria deJesus and Gertie Nevels will be ordinary and the enactment of individual talent a social expectation. And that time has come!

7. Human Sexuality and Mutuality

BEVERLY WILDUNG HARRISON

We Christians know very little about our own history with respect to human sexuality, especially its seamier side. We must acknowledge this history before we move to embrace fine platitudes about the possibilities of human gender relationships.[1] Otherwise we will be compromising a liberation theological hermeneutic by making contemporary Christian morality look better than it is or has been. In this connection, *Power and Sexuality*, a much neglected book by patristics scholar Samuel Laeuchli, is helpful. It is a study of one Church Council—the Council of Elvira, in Granada (now Spain), held in the year 309. This study discloses how and why the Christian tradition got into such trouble about human sexuality. "The Christian church, as the anti-heretical literature shows in chapter after chapter, always tried to discredit its rivals as sexually inferior, an apologetic slander technique that has worked to this day."[2] In a time when that slander technique works only with those already frightened and vulnerable from other sources, it is time to ask, "Where have we gone wrong?"

CHRISTIANITY'S LEGACY OF HUMAN SEXUALITY AND GENDER RELATIONS

The problem, I submit, is the pervasive sex-negativity and fear of the power of sexuality in the Christian tradition.

Beverly Wildung Harrison is professor of social ethics at Union Theological Seminary in New York City. In her research, writing, and teaching, she specializes in feminist theology, ethics and sexuality, and economic justice. She is the author of *Our Right to Choose: Toward a New Ethic of Abortion*, and a forthcoming book is entitled *Making the Connection: Essays in Feminist Social Ethics*.

In his fine book, *Embodiment: An Approach to Sexuality and Christian Theology*,[3] James Nelson ponders the sources of sex-negativity in our tradition. Nelson contends that two dualisms have embedded themselves deeply in Christian thought and perception. One is the spiritualistic dualism which conceives of persons as body *and* spirit (or as body *and* mind), not as a unity but as an uneasy amalgam. Nelson rightly observes that such dualism had no place in the Hebraic spirituality which we Christians purport to honor in our appropriation of the ancient Hebrew scriptures. But such dualism was a virulent force, characteristic of the terribly religious culture of late Hellenism into which Christianity was born. Nor was its influence on Christian perception of the world slow to emerge, as any reading of second century theologians such as Justin Martyr, Tatian, Origen and Tertullian makes clear. Furthermore, the growing attraction of asceticism in early Christian theology attests an escalating revulsion to the body as the source of temptation and evil. So "inferior" are bodily functions to many of the church fathers that "sex" is justified only for procreation. Procreative functionalism eventually became *the* meaning of sex in the Christian tradition, and for many influential theologians, such as Jerome, it was a very dubious necessity, literally justified only because through sex, more virgins and rigorous ascetic Christians might be born.[4]

The full force of Christian sex-negativism cannot be understood, however, without recognizing the interconnection between the spiritualistic dualism, with its antisexual and anti-body bias, and that other dualism, gender dualism in which, male is superior to female. The concrete, historical-social relations between men and women in Christian history has constituted an oppressive praxis which shapes our theology. It is a truism of feminist analysis that in Western tradition, women have symbolized sexuality, animal nature, and body. Whether in the appalling biology of classical Hellenic philosophers like Aristotle, or in the teachings of the church fathers, women, unless committed to asceticism, and unqualifiedly "pious," are evil. "Woman's god-given role" is either to be dutiful and faithful mothers, or virginal ascetics. In fact, in the ascetic tradition, a woman *became a man* by renouncing her "natural" inclinations through rigorous ascetic practice. By a *self-effacing* piety, a woman, literally, became spiritual, overcoming her inherent blot as sexual temptress and her pure physicality by spirituality.

It goes without saying that male gender superiority, in its theological form as masculinist idolatry, is older than Christianity. Over fifteen thousand years of history, the institutions of male control of women's reality, have evolved. We know now, thanks to feminist scholarship in anthropology and history, that there has been a great diversity in the sorts of institutions and social controls elaborated to keep women "in our place," and to construe male reality as *normatively* human. Because of this scholarship, however, we also know how deeply the central institutions of dominant religions are implicated in the legitimation of male superiority. Sociologist of religion Nancy Jay has demonstrated that numerous human religious systems, including Christianity, have developed blood sacrifice rituals which aim to replace human once-bornness of women by twice-bornness through a male deity.[5] Of course, it is true that the ancient Hebrews did not invent patriarchy—in its concrete and original sociological form, the ownership of women and children by "the father"—nor were the dominant Christian fathers exceptionally creative amongst the intellectual elites of their day in embracing the ideal of sexual transactions with women as characteristic animality which wars with genuine spirituality, and of women as the source not only of sexual temptation but of evil itself. But what the now massive and growing work of feminist scholarship forces us to confront is the lingering disvaluation of women which lives on in the praxis—that is, both the theological reflection and the practice—of Christians. And remember, only the *good* women—that is, women *more* consistently self-sacrificing and ascetic than men—were celebrated in the church.

The usual theological response among Christian theologians to these facts are either to trivialize the matter, labeling so-called "women's issues" as of lesser import to the "real" issues of justice, as if the well-being of 51 percent of the human race had nothing to do with justice, or to reject them outright, as grounded in overwrought feminist mutterings. There are even suggestions that feminism threatens to reintroduce Canaanite Baal cults or other pagan practices into the seamless web of Christian tradition. Since feminists have all but concluded anyway that many heresies were to become so precisely because, in one way or another, they challenged these dualisms in which the Orthodox were so embedded, the flip dismissal of feminist critiques only reinforces our suspicions or—in the case of Christian feminists —fears that Christianity may really be intrinsically a system of male deification.

We Protestants, not least we Reformed Christians, continue to believe that we have largely overcome these dualisms. Far too readily we wrap ourselves in self-congratulation that the Reformation broke the hold of these baleful dynamics of sexual asceticism through Protestant Christian history. After all, the ending of clerical celibacy proves this, does it not? To be sure, the Reformers, none more passionately than Calvin, embraced marriage almost as a duty. (Reviewing the civil ordinances of early Calvinist Geneva for my research on my book on abortion reminded me of how passionately Calvin and his cohorts believed that marriage *was* a duty. I would add that it had to be, for if men must marry women, whom they view as deficient in humanity, the external rule of "duty" necessarily must be invoked.)

The truth is that nothing in the Reformation can be read as a genuine reversal of this negative antisexual, antifemale, antisensuality heritage. Luther and Calvin celebrated in the nobility of "the good woman," but that was nothing new in Christian history. In fact, it was a mere reassertion of social convention. They revisaged the role of sexuality in marriage as involving *more* than procreation, but that was because marriage was so pivotal to their view of divine-human relations. We miss the problematic of current discussion if we do not also acknowledge that the Reformers embedded the marital relationship, and especially the child-centered family, as the central, sacralizing institution of "the household of faith."

Nor did the Reformation strengthen women's social role in society. The Reformers—as our Catholic feminist sisters remind us regularly—closed down women's religious houses, destroying the one clear institutional base of women's culture in the late Middle Ages. The Reformers and their followers did nothing to change women's role in the church. Futhermore, as historian Trevor-Roper reminds us, their followers joined the rising tide of witch-hunting, the great European witch craze,[6] which was *premodern* Christian Europe's most organized and systematic bout with *internal* genocide. (The same period sees the external genocidal pattern of "domestication" of Africans by Europeans through the slave system.)

Until forced to change, then, the mainstream churches of the Reformation were, like the Catholic tradition before it, institutions which assumed that full spirituality and theological power resided with males. I have elsewhere observed the anomaly of the Christian church, which encouraged male-male bonding so powerfully, also having to support marriage—that is, intimacy relations with social inferiors—as its central institution. I truly believe that homophobia in our churches is directly related to the powerful sublimated eroticism of a Christian tradition so fixated on masculinist symbols, which also demand normative heterosexuality as its sexual norm.

In any case, the praxis of Protestant Christianity on these matters did not change in the centuries following because of any internal theological innovation. Such constructive change as there has been has come painfully and reluctantly, through confrontation with the historical justice movements of women in Western culture which call for conditions for women's fuller humanity. The emergence of gay movements have accelerated that pressure.

Even the most progressive of our theologians responded reluctantly, while the church deflected feminist calls for justice by adopting the nineteen century bourgeois romantic view that women are nobler and *morally* superior to men, the true mediators of nurturance and moral uplift, and are to be revered (read: pedestalized and patronized). Elsewhere I have documented the fact that in the early nineteenth century, it was still possible for Reformation theologians to speak of women chiefly under the image of Eve and the fall. By the end of the century, women in the church had been elevated to the other side of the traditional dualism—the devoted, mothering, virginally asexual "good woman," the only woman to whom Christianity had been able to relate.

In Reformed theology, even in its most progressive expressions, sexuality still remains shrouded in the mystifications of either "God-given" or "natural" existence. Whether in the theology of Emil Brunner who lapses into natural law thinking under the rubric of "orders" or Barth's biblicist and silly exegesis of female "voluntary" subordination to male,[7] women, sexuality, and marriage are treated within an *essentially* ahistorical, acultural horizon. In spite of the *celebration* of the historicity of existence in Reformed theology, when these issues are before us, all are still treated either as paradigms for *direct divine* decree or "natural" determination.

Such a state of affairs, however, simply will not do. In our own time these mystifications about ahistorical sexuality are being unmasked, and if the church does not change, our theology will, more and more, be rightly judged to be intrinsically intertwined with the mystifications of masculinist deification. Any communion which still rests so uneasy with human sexuality and with gender justice that it feels reluctant about contraception—which has, after all, made a major contribution to delivering women from what has been through history, a source of unspeakable capriciousness and suffering for most women—still has a long road to travel before public confession will be transformed by evidence of liberating praxis.

RESOURCES FOR A NEW PARADIGM

THE RISING CONSCIOUSNESS OF WOMEN

It is the presumption of liberation hermeneutics that contradictions within the praxis of the community of faith will be recognized most clearly, and challenged, by those whose lives are negatively affected by and marginated because of these contradictions. Not surprisingly then, the implications of our assumptions about gender relations and human sexuality are being challenged today chiefly by women. Those like myself, mostly white, educated, of the "middle strata" of this society, have experienced the taken-for-granted views of sexuality and gender relations embedded in Christianity as a direct invitation to our own subjugation as persons. Unlike racial and ethnic women and poor women, who are the majority of all women, we escape the double and triple jeopardy of racist and class oppression. We experience gender subjugation, even if sometimes subtly, as a pattern of marginalization and trivialization unintwined with other oppressions. We are the ones who, given the "pedesta-lism" of bourgeois life, have been socialized to believe that our sexuality exists only through our relations to and dependency upon men. We are those who have been invited, at the cost of loss of personal power, to deny that we are "Our Bodies, Our-selves."[8] It is not surprising, then, that the book by this title, written by a Woman's Health Collective, has been high on the list of works targeted by the New Religious Right for removal from school libraries. This volume, predicated upon the assump-tions of the newer feminist perspectives on sexuality and read by countless thousands of women, is but one of a vast library of works that contemporary women have written on matters re-lated to the issue of sexuality and gender relations. Through these works women are invited to re-vision our own being as self-directed, sensuous body-selves, as those who can and must direct our self-expression as sexual beings who are responsible *agents.* As body-selves, sensuous centers of self-direction and relation-ship, our lives and sexuality are ourselves, intrinsic aspects of our being, and we bear responsibility for the choices we make in terms both of sensuality and relationship.

The empowering self-respect which has followed upon wom-en's discoveries around issues of sexuality has, I submit, been the generating source of the new courage and activism of many women in these difficult times. For a woman to recognize herself as an embodied psychosexual, spiritual unity, means for her to see that she is an embodied self, not merely that she *has* as body. This means, among other things, that *all* our relations to oth-ers—to God, to neighbor, to cosmos—is mediated through our bodies, which are the locus of our perception and knowledge of the world. Our senses—*all* our senses, including touch—medi-ate the manifold world to us. We are not split, "compounds" of mind and emotion, or body and spirit. Our emotions mediate our basic interactions with the world. Our minds are an integrat-ed aspect of our body systems, shaped by the matrix of our sen-suous being in the world.

SEXUALITY IN THIS PARADIGM

The discovery that our sexuality is intrinsic to who we are, that we are sexual beings whose bodies ground *all* our relations to the world, that we are not merely "sexual" through genital contact with males, has helped feminists make sense of the dynamics of sexual subjugation throughout recorded history. It has also led us to perceive that, with bodily repression comes *loss of a sense of our connectedness* to the rest of nature, to the cosmos, and to each other. From this perspective it becomes clear that "individualism"—a sense of the self as genuinely autonomous and independent, experienced as unrelated existent—is the result of *misunderstanding* who we are as persons. While the equation of "person" with "individual" is not uncommon, such an equation is based upon misconception. A person, as Reformed theologian John MacMurray rightly argued,[9] is a *richly related,* centered being, one whose ties to others are deep and complexly rich. To be *fully* a person is to be *deeply related to others.*

In this newer paradigm, then, our sexuality is not a "segment" of our reality. Our sexuality is our total, embodied, sensuous connection to all things, as female or as male. Because our embodied sensuousness is the ground of our being in the world, it is also foundational to our sense of well-being, and to our "power of relation" in and to the world. Furthermore, as we move beyond body/mind and body/spirit dualism, we discover that our own well-being and our relationships to others are not dualistic or antagonistic alternatives. Personal well-being and deeply grounded relationship to others are *intimately interstructured possibilities.* This means, literally, that who I am in my "power of relation"[10] determines and is determined by my relationships, and that my well-being and that of the others to whom I am related depends foundationally on existing conditions of mutual respect between us or upon the lack thereof. Women have been learning this lesson of *mutual* empowerment, for we have been, literally, "hearing each other into speech."[11] We have been *taking ourselves and each other seriously,* as those who have the power to "name" reality, especially in those areas where men infrequently have heard us or taken us seriously.

All of us, then, literally call forth each other in relationship, and our power of being and capacity to act emerges through our sensuous interaction in relation. If our modes of relationship are not grounded in bodily integrity, and if our ways of being with each other preclude mutuality—which is the power, simultaneously, *to affect and be affected by another*—we cannot and will not have *either* personal well-being *or* community, which is to say, relations of mutuality, shared empowerment, and common respect.

"Mutuality" has been downgraded in our theological tradition, and portrayed as a lesser good than "agape"—unrequited radical, divine love. But in a feminist paradigm, mutuality, or genuine reciprocity, is utterly foundational. There is nothing "higher." Without it, we are thwarted, broken beings, those who seek to avoid vulnerability—that is, the *capacity to be deeply affected by another*. Furthermore—and this is critical for our ethics—the absence of such genuine bodily integrity and mutual vulnerability leads to a distortion in our power of agency, that is, our capacity to act and be acted upon. Far from being a peripheral secondary or poor approximation of love, bodily integrity, self-respect, and *mutuality* are of love's essence. When they are present in relationship, that relationship evokes simultaneously self-enhancement and community or deep intimacy. Whenever one party is invulnerable, and therefore unwilling or unable to be affected by another, there is and can be no love present. And wherever bodily integrity is not respected, genuine other-regardingness is absent. How we relate as body-selves is paradigmatic of how we experience and express power.

Parenthetically, I should add that neither our Christian ethics nor our later, secular moral traditions in the West do justice to the concern of bodily integrity as foundational to our moral relations to each other. Consider, for example, our notions of human rights. Our liberal political traditions value, as foundational human rights, those conditions of relationship which already presuppose the basic, concrete conditions of physical well-being. We do *not* see food, shelter, and freedom from bodily control by another as moral requirements of a good society. This is no accident or mere oversight, for our political constitutions were written, and interpreted by, men who owned slaves, who were not disturbed by a praxis which included ownership of other human beings, and who used black women's bodies as breeders of "property." These same men also did not see any contradiction in denying the rights of citizenship, and therefore the signs of full humanity, to the women with whom they shared their beds, who bore the children carrying their names. Because of these, and other patterns of praxis that negate the full humanity of people, our liberal political and moral traditions do not *ground* human rights as basic conditions of well-being concretely enough, in a fashion that recognizes the basic embodiedness of humanity, and that acknowledges our basic relatedness as embodied, species-beings.

THE "PROBLEM" OF SEXUALITY IN THE FEMINIST PARADIGM

Given this understanding of ourselves as sexual beings—sensuous and related—the problem is not that there is too much sex per se. The fact is that we have very little sex which enhances our self-respect and sense of well-being, and simultaneously deepens our relations to each other. The truth is that we cannot have one without the other—deeper self-respect and deeper intimacy. We have little of either in this society. For all our society's preoccupations with genital sexuality, there is little evidence that the result is a greater sense of playfulness, genuine tenderness, enhanced human communication.

In a feminist paradigm, our sexuality is problematic because it is entangled not only in the old dualisms but in distorted patterns of power-in-relation. Women, especially, are "objectified," understood not as full human sexual beings, but as sex objects who exist to fulfill male needs and are evaluated as idealized projections of that need. As sex object, a woman is to live as mediator of sensuality and affective support to men. But now men are also entering into objectification, living by "the looking glass effect"—that is, seeing themselves *through the eyes* of a purported lover. Objectified sexuality invites us to experience ourselves *chiefly* as objects of another, to experience sexuality as a power relationship in which we enmesh an other in seductive dependency or place ourselves in that position. To experience the *power* of relationship, there must be reciprocity, shared power, power exhibiting co-creative, mutually enhancing action. In the dominant paradigm of sexuality and gender relations, power emerges as control of another, whether as seduction, manipulation, or coercion. To be sexually valued means, too often, to have the other in our power or to "give over" our power of relation to another. Dynamics of ownership, control or "possession" permeate our sexual relations. We speak of "scoring" or "making it" or "getting what we want" from the sexual partner.

I do not mean to say, however, that the problem of sexuality is merely the consequence of "bad," objectified *attitudes* about sex. Sexual objectification is not merely a matter of individual sensibility. The truth is that, in this society, our expectations about sexuality are overburdened because patterns of objectification and alienation are so widespread in our broader social relationships. Mutually enhancing, intimate, vulnerable relationships are rare in *any* dimension of our social relations. Our advanced capitalist economic system conditions us to experience all aspects of ourselves, including our bodily sensuous labor, as "commodities" to be bought and sold. For the most part, people in this society have given up the expectation that work will enhance their self-respect, or that the power of relation will be expressed in the work they do. Instead we see our work as a means to an end, as a means to economic security and to consumption. We should not forget that the two intellectuals who so deeply changed our world, Marx and Freud, both agreed upon what it means to be a full human being. To be whole, they argued, we need to be able to love well and to work well. In the expression of our eros and our power to create through sensuous labor, we express our personal power, meeting the power of relation others extend. When we encounter these others as willing our good and respond willing their well-being, the "realm of God"—the power of relation—is released and mutual well-being enhanced.

The growing sense of powerlessness of large numbers of people in the middle strata of this society is no chimera. Increasingly, we do *not* have the power of self-direction or mutuality in our lives. Again, we do *not* have one without the other. In such a situation, where alienation and objectification or the commoditization of life is widespread, our anxieties grow, and the sense of something gone awry increases. However, the liberal ideology of this society, what Michael Lewis calls "the individual as central sensibility,"[12] prevents us from seeing and naming the problem. In such a context, we project our anxieties outward and "blame the victims"[13]—those even more exploited and vulnerable than ourselves. Witness the rising racism of our society, now "respectable" once again. And as economic exploitation increases, our society is rife with growing class antagonisms that we do not have even the conceptual frame to recognize. Resentments are expressed at every turn, but we do not see the connections between people's growing "asocial" actions and the dynamics of our political-economic order.

In the midst of all of this, the New Right seeks, consciously, to blame our social dis-ease upon the women's movement, and gay men and lesbians. Uppity women and gays are, we are told, undermining traditional order. The use of sexuality issues in New Right propaganda is an organized response armed to exploit the widespread anxiety people are experiencing.[14] These strategies help to deflect discontent and to keep those who actually are in control safe and secure from scrutiny and accountability to the rest of us whose lives are shaped by their decisions.

In the face of all of this—the reality of growing powerlessness, the anxieties of things amiss in the society—people retreat from the so-called "public" world of political and economic relations, turning to the "private" sphere—that is, to primary, intimacy relations to ground that sense of personal well-being missing elsewhere. Our expectations for our intimacy relations are *enormous*, and, too often, these turn out to be too tender a need to sustain our self-respect adequately. We seek meaning, desperately, in interpersonal relations and expect our intimacy relations to deliver us from the loss of personal empowerment and self-respect suffered in other areas of our lives. We bring incredible expectations to our love relations with another, and for the most part, we are often bitterly disappointed. Our problem with sex amidst all of this is *not* that we have so much of it, but that it is joyless, so earnest, so lacking playfulness and refreshment. Such overloaded sex does not participate in growing intimacy; it often exacerbates objectification.

We Christians have had a hand in increasing the pressures on sexual relationships, especially in marriage. By insisting that we are to be fully sexual only in marriage, by teaching people to expect so much of their primary intimacy commitments, and to see their life partners as *the* mediating source of sexuality and intimacy, we have romanticized marriage, and denied people a sense of their own sexual integrity. We have even taught sexual repression, for if one is to deny sexuality and sensuousness except in a marital context, one learns to "shut off" sensuousness and sexual feeling. And when sexuality is denied and repressed, our sensuousness does not "go away." Sexual feeling denied re-emerges, sometimes as compulsive sexual behavior, or as misdirected or compulsive need, and sex appears as a "foreign power," outside of ourselves, as a dangerous force which must "be controlled."

This romanticization of marriage and the family within the church must stop. Honesty requires us to begin to recognize that the American family is a battleground, where rape, battering, incest and child abuse abound. Marital relations which actually involve tender sensuality and deep mutual respect are *very* rare among us. We are a needy people, a people who are *not* sensuous, or at ease with sensuality, but are those who use each other in a futile effort to enhance self-respect at the cost of another's sense of self. Men whose lives are thwarted in the workplace go home to express their sense of powerlessness and frustration through violence and coercion toward their wives and children. Needy adults exploit psychically vulnerable children to experience the sensuality they do not and cannot express in adult relations. In this situation, divorces frequently are not "forgivable failures." Just as often they are exemplifications of real maturity, a step in the process of reordering relations in the direction of self-respect and mutuality.

And even that symptom of sexual disorder with which I have some sympathy—the exploitation of sex and pornography—is more symptom than cause of this disease. It is important to recognize that pornography is not wrong because it is erotic. It is wrong because it is predicated upon an exploitative power of relation, one where women, and some men, are portrayed as objects of conquests, or as temptresses who long to be "taken" and controlled. Furthermore, pornography is *very* big business, and we will not be rid of it so long as there is profit to be made by it. In a sense, pornography is the ultimate displacement of sensual, mutual relationship by objectified fantasy. Many are more turned on by watching than by concrete sensuous transactions expressing love.

TOWARD A NEW PARADIGM OF SEXUALITY

The implications of all this for the church, its theology and ethics of sexuality are immense, but I can only highlight a few implications here. We must face up to the extent to which Christianity has been implicated in antisensual, antiwomen praxis, and how much our Christian teaching on sexuality has contributed to sexual repression, sexual objectification, and to legitimating marriage as a form of institutional control of women's sexuality.

The controversies over the role of women, and more especially gay people, are, I believe, intimately connected with defense of the old paradigm. The effort to entrench Christianity as the defender of the institution of normative heterosexuality is part and parcel of the effort to require conformity to the old paradigm of human sexuality. And in all of this, Christians project on to gay people unfaced anxieties about sexuality. As nonconformists to the social norm, gay men and lesbians are perceived as "really sexual," as those who express sensuality and embodied sexuality without constraint. Such projections must cease, and we must find our way to valuing, celebrating, making normative, all deep, respectful, sensuous, empowering relationships, which, wherever they exist, ground our well-being and the bonds of mutual respect.

We must learn, together, that coming to terms with our embodied sensuous capacity for relationship—that is, our sexuality—is a condition for freeing ourselves from patterns of compulsive and controlling sex so widespread in our churches. To come to terms with our sexuality means to reappropriate sex as a vital, delightful dimension of our sexuality, but also as a dimension without our self-control.

Since our sensuality is the ground of our transactions with the world, it is also the foundation of our creativity, our spontaneity, our power to affect and be affected by each other. A disembodied faith and a disembodied church are without sensuality, spontaneity, and creativity. A church which denies the positive reality of sexuality is dead, ponderous, boring, and unable to touch people's souls. I believe we have paid a high price for our evasions of human sexuality. I see to much banality, superficiality of feeling, and a lack of deep sensibility and emotional responsiveness in our churches. We are out of touch with the depth of life, the concrete sufferings, and the vulnerability of people. Furthermore, the almost morbid fear of conflict among us, related as I believe to our denial of sensuality, endangers us far more than any specific conflict could. The price we pay for this fear of conflict is lifelessness, and the impairment of our power of relation. We fear the growing "spiritual power" of the rising evangelical groups on the one hand, but stumble to ape them on the other. At the same time, we cut ourselves off from those who are experiencing *new sensuous empowerment* through liberative struggle. Racial and ethnic people who struggle for justice for their communities, strong women, gay people, and all those who have left sexual repression behind, do *not feel welcome in our churches,* and these are the ones who are "coming of age," critically, in our social world, no longer willing to "please" the established powers in society.

All of this also has deep implications for our theological understanding. Ours is a tradition in which the relationship between God and God's people has been understood, too often, as precluding reciprocal power-in-relation. God as God-self is too often understood in our tradition as *one invulnerable in relation to us.* By contrast, a feminist paradigm evokes recognition that an invulnerable deity would, necessarily, be one who objectified us, who rules us by external control. This is not the God we meet in relation.

From a liberation theology perspective, our relationship to God is intrinsically shaped through our relationships to each other. Our social relations are not separable from our God-relations. To speak of social relations is already to speak of God-relations, and any conception of God-relations already implies patterns of social relations. The normative role of justice, right relationship, to our theology means that we understand that in making right relations God's power is disclosed. Gustavo Gutierrez[15] has argued that, literally, justice reveals the face of God. I have learned from him to understand that when a society gives up the struggle to do justice, to make right our disordered relations, we *literally lose a living vision of God.*

I believe that this society is *profoundly* atheistic, precisely because we are losing concern for the struggle for justice. In such a world, we Reformed theologians may proclaim "the mighty Acts of God" and "God's prevenient power" to the high heavens— and no one will believe us! For when we no longer experience the depth of our power of agency, when our longing to act toward each other in search of right relationship atrophies, *we are cut off from God's power*, which is not objectified power, separate from us, but the power-of-relation in our midst. This power of God draws us to each other in common commitment, and into the struggle to embody our co-humanity mutually, that is, toward shared well-being. When we cut ourselves off from those who are now engaging this struggle, we say "no" to God. And in such a situation, surrogate, disembodied, dualistic spiritualities emerge, tempting us to forms of withdrawal from the real, sensuous life that is God's gift to us. In such a situation, "love" becomes not the power to act faithfully and loyally toward another, but a sentiment, an isolated feeling, to be manipulated to secure our invulnerability to mutual relationship. To be a Christian comes to mean that one wears a plastic smile and passes out palliatives, theological and psychological, to kill the searing pain which rends our world.

By contrast to this manipulative spirituality, which purchases "spiritual security" at the price of evasion of reality, we Christians require a deep, subtle understanding of our spiritual situation. In this situation we need a conception of our ethical responsibility that evokes our calling as God's people, not under the rubric of mere "obedience,"[16]—for "obedience" is always conformity to the *external* rule and order of another—but under the images of discernment and creative praxis. We are called to find *new* patterns of relationship, fresh ways of being with and for each other, in the struggle for justice. In the past, those who have called us to join the struggle for justice have too often implied that doing justice is a stern task, a joyless demand, a requirement or obligation which must necessarily lead us to turn our back on our own well-being. But this way of viewing justice presents us with a false portrait of reality. To reach out to each other, to struggle for rich relationship, to accept our *common co-humanity*, does not require us to renounce our own well-being, but to begin to find its authentic ground and depth, in the joyful discovery of the richness that comes through deep relation. To be sure, the human costs of the struggle for justice are high, and many are called upon to give of themselves radically, even unto death. But those who love justice, and have their passion lovingly shaped toward right relation, act not because they are enamored of sacrifice. Rather, they are moved by a love strong enough to sustain their action for right relation, even unto death.

In this regard we Christians have, I believe, even misunderstood the praxis of him whom we name as "Lord." Jesus' paradigmatic role in the story of our salvation rests not in his willingness to sacrifice himself, but in his passionate love of right relations and his refusal to cease to embody the power-of-relation in the face of that which would thwart it. It was his refusal to desist from radical love, not a preoccupation with sacrifice, which makes his work irreplaceable.

We are called of God to *life abundant*, and in the struggle for justice we discover that genuine abundance of life comes from embodying a solidarity with one another which is deeply mutual, which is to say, reciprocal. We need desperately to learn that it is the struggle for justice itself which empowers us to learn to dance together, celebrating in anticipating, the co-humanity into which we are called. In solidarity born of the struggle for justice, we can joyfully live, empowered, toward those right relationships in which *all* may know that abundant life is the birthright of those God brings to life. The path of justice is often costly, but it is always, also, the path to discovering, through the sharing of our co-humanity, how good and real is the sensuous, embodied life God gives.

8. Re-membering: A Global Perspective on Women

CONSTANCE F. PARVEY

Behind the issues raised in this chapter are questions and partial answers. Why a new consciousness among women now? Is solidarity among women possible, or are we loyal first to class, race, country, church and economic status, and only after these to other women? Can the women's movement bridge the gap between women? Are we still, as women in the church, trying to enter the mainstream? If this goal is possible at all—or even desirable—how long will it take? Does the pyramid of power, male controlled, exert too overwhelming a hold over political, economic, educational, and church life? Are there enough women ready to challenge the fact that our place in the ordering of power is symbolic, no matter where we are positioned as individuals? Are we willing to pay the price for self-empowerment—conflict, taking stands, public exposure? Is it possible for enough women and men to be converted that we can start afresh in institutional life, using models of partnership that are mutually empowering and for which justice and love are ethical norms?

These questions unfold in the pages that follow. The issues raised push the reader toward the larger global narrative of

Constance F. Parvey is a research scholar at the Center for Research on Women at Wellesley College. Prior to assuming her present position, she was visiting lecturer in theology and church history at the Vancouver School of Theology. For three years she directed a study on the Community of Women and Men in the Church while on the staff of the World Council of Churches. Dr. Parvey has also pastored a Lutheran church in Cambridge, Massachusetts, and was chaplain at Harvard University and the Massachusetts Institute of Technology. Her books include *The Community of Women and Men in the Church* and *Ordination of Women in Ecumenical Perspective.*

women's lives, unfettered by individual experiences. Visions for a new humanity cannot be separated from women's contexts: women vis-à-vis other women, women vis-à-vis men, women vis-à-vis institutions dominated by men and by male polities. Only as these contexts of power and power relationships are transformed can a new humanity become more than vision; yet this is not merely material for dreams but a necessity for human survival. This chapter is an act of re-membering. To re-member is not only to ask when and where, but also why? It is a theological word; it recalls God's covenant and is the ancient way of learning to keep it; it is a pivotal word in worship. What follows is a re-membering of women in global context.

Why is a consciousness, a sensibility freshly expressed, emerging worldwide among women—East, West, North, South, rich and poor, women from dominating and oppressed classes? Why is there so much speaking openly about women's positions and roles, about exploitation of women and, among women in some places, about the little hope, the little space? This is one of those immense questions to which there is no one answer, yet it is essential to listen and to respond. Why now? Why is it this moment in history that so many more women are emboldened to speak and to write about themselves, to engage in confrontational dialogue with men and with other women about how they understand themselves, how they have been misunderstood and its consequences, and what enters into the content of their hopes and dreams for living more *holos*,[1] more of the wholeness, entireness, of human life?

Some voices, male and female, would say that this is an exercise in futility, such a desire is unrealistic; it is an escape into another world that is an unattainable realm. Women today, these voices say, are trying to reach for too much, their hopes are too high, lacking the pragmatism necessary for the "real world." No one can deny that these new sensibilities exist; one finds them everywhere—women risking, speaking, asking fundamental questions, boldly making what seem to be impossible assertions, daring to move toward goals that change the world and its dominant images.

DIFFERENT EXPECTATIONS

The ground under conventional man/woman relationships is shifting; the old equilibrium is dis-established, and as yet there is no certain new foundation. Ours is a time of insecurity for both women and men. For many women, not all, this insecurity gives rise to hope, to new self-understandings and self-empowerment. It is the dawning of an exciting time. It is a "getting-out-from-under" time as women make their exodus from the socialization that has considered them as "second best" or as meant for something "not-quite-as-good." For many women this is a psychological/spiritual springtime, a time for shedding old skin, old armoring, a time for planting in order to grow, for dying in order to rise again. Yet, for women-and-men relationships, this is a troublesome for-the-time-being, because the societal structures and behavior patterns have not yet made a parallel shift. Men who are partners with this change sometimes get mixed signals from women; women, too, are disappointed by the difficulties of maintaining solidarity with other women. For men it is hard to find other men who are willing to talk about what the new identities of women mean for them, how they need to change and discover different foundations and psychological/spiritual resources within themselves. Some—women and men—in this uncertain transition time become more defensive. "Why should *I* change?" they ask.

As I see the women and men students around me, I see that they too are ambivalent. Young women students at the university where I teach assume that they are addressed as women, not girls. They are less dependent on the regular "date," more comfortable with each other's company, even on weekend nights. The screaming Tuesdays, when the dates for the weekend used to be lined up, now hardly exist. Women and men students visit back and forth as they would in a big household. They appear to share more familial life with one another. In terms of roles, the women are more athletic—they run and are in more team sports; occasionally the men will bake bread or cookies. Many work side by side in commerce and law courses and in science laboratories. There are still times reminiscent of the behavior of "old-college-days," but the social hysteria is lessened. These students seem to like each other, enjoy each other, and from time to time, they even fall in love.

But does this one example of educated, affluent students function as an indicator for a universal phenomenon? Yes and no. The yes underlines the fact that student relationships with each other are changing. They seem to value friendships among both sexes and cultivate them; they care about their basic community life, its quality and all persons in it. The no has to do with a qualification, with the recognition that student life is a position of privilege, part of the suspended state between protected childhood and the public world of labor and work. Though economically and politically women students face an uncertain future, they have a range of choices—to go on to graduate or professional school, to marry or not, to have children or not, to develop a friendship into a sexual relationship, to develop friendships around common goals and interests, to delay marriage, to marry now and begin a family, or to live as single adults. Like their older sisters in the affluent sectors of North Atlantic countries, they are expecting to work and to be treated equally. They look at career choices, having in mind the motives of success and achievement, but also aware of the obstacles. For the most part, young women today see themselves as becoming fully participating citizens in their own right. Whether they chose traditional roles as wives and mothers, or new professional roles, or some combination, they expect to be treated as equal persons. They are not interested in men who try to put them down or in work where they are locked into jobs without growth. Young women today are already guardians of their own space, and the young men feel it. These young people are part of growing generations of youth whose mothers have begun to set a different pace for their daughters and some for their sons as well. Until now they have not encountered the working world, or the demands that it puts on roles and family life, but they do know that they have an enlarged social expectation of themselves that they must pursue. They are part of that slow revolution of consciousness for which the work structures of society are not yet ready. Taking equality for granted, they have yet to face the inequalities, visible and invisible, and the accompanying loneliness that are consequences of structural inequities that separate women's and men's lives.

EQUALITY AND HIERARCHY

In Eastern Europe, sisters and brothers live in a quite different situation. In countries like the German Democratic Republic (East Germany) or Romania, which found themselves socialist countries overnight, the societal structure changed dramatically. Women were suddenly thrown into partnership with men in a man's culture based on a combination of quasi-feudalist and new socialist ideals. Overnight, women were declared equal—without a struggle. Today they are paid equally for equal work. In such a setting they are asking questions about what it means to be a woman. For the women in the Soviet Union who wrote their own women's almanac,[2] feminist issues revolved around the right to be feminine, the right to preserve some of women's traditionally held values, women's traditional images, even in religion. To the Western eye, this appears akin to the "total woman." The feminism of some of these Russian sisters may sound strange to sisters in the West, but it is significant as part of the wider movement of women who are speaking from within their own situations, in this case even risking their citizenship in order to publish their magazine.

Women in the German Democratic Republic enjoy their new freedom and space.[3] If given the choice of working or not working, most would choose to work, because it gives them a participatory role in public life. Some wish that the overarching patriarchal attitudes would change more, that men too would take up more of the responsibility for the household, for parenting, and for family relationships. If husbands do not keep their side of the partnership alive, women can divorce; they are not dependent on the men as breadwinners. Economic independence means that women find that they can manage work and home life without a partner, although it is not easy. Large numbers of women choose not to marry, creating a lively women's culture of single working women—the bottom of the hierarchy of preference—as one woman put it. The high priority of the society appears to be the married working woman with children. The second is the divorced mother with children, the third is the unmarried woman with children, and the fourth is the unmarried woman without children. Perhaps there is truth as well in the statement that for women not to marry, not to have children, is the ultimate protest against the values of the patriarchal society or state. Women the world over, with few exceptions, are identified through their male relationships; they are mothers of X, wives of Y, and daughters of J. To be known by one's autonomous identity is a statement in itself—even if not consciously articulated.

In cultures where women have had a central economic role—market women in parts of Africa, for example, and weavers among some Indian cultures in Latin America—women's status is diminished when modern macroeconomic structures intrude and dominate local economies.[4] With the growth of militarism worldwide and fifty-four countries classified by a recent United Nations study as military dictatorships,[5] the roles of women become even more vulnerable and dependent—at all class levels. Wherever military priorities take over, it is mainly men who benefit in status, salary, power; thus the gap between women and men widens. Sex tourism often accompanies this, making the situation worse, as is apparent in the Ermila Bar district of Manila, in the Philippines, where eleven- and twelve-year-olds who support families from money earned as street prostitutes, are walking carriers and sufferers of herpes, syphilis and gonorrhea.[6] Woman power wielded as a force for peace, is an inevitable—almost an unconscious impulse—in response to this degradation. Large masses of women not only oppose the violence and potential violence unleashed by military power; they also oppose the violence and potential violence against themselves and against their children as militarism destroys the social fabric. Violence takes many forms, but it is always characterized by the increasing dependence of the most vulnerable partner and the increasing authoritarianism of the dominating partner. Militarism is manifested as "power over" and when that power is frustrated, it is often domestically targeted against women and children.

CATCHING UP AND LOSING GROUND

The posttechnological world view is informed by the ideology that it will be a new era for women. The assumption is that women can be as competent with computers as men. Women can use them for the same value-free purposes—programming a tank across the Arabian desert, or a commuter train between Tokyo and Kyoto. But what about the millions of women and men who are marginalized by the mainstream of modern technocratic culture? There exists a myth that women ought to be educated into the skills of technocracy so that they are not left behind. That they are left behind is not a myth. Perhaps women are already too far behind; perhaps only a few elites will ever catch up. What about the millions of others not so educated, privileged, "intelligent"? They also have rights, desires, gifts, and responsibilities. Is much of the work that women have done now obsolete? For example, will African market women who control traditional economies have to retrain or be left behind? Will Indian agricultural women have to learn modern farming, animal husbandry, and finance, or also be left behind? Working women everywhere are more and more aware of the impact of global technological and economic factors on their self-determination, but they are much less aware of how to cope with the change, how to keep from losing the little ground they now have.[7]

THE "ONE AND THE MANY"

In fact, women's participation in postmodern technocracy engenders an apparently irreconcilable conflict. Women, like men in technological cultures who evidence leadership, are now being told that they must be an integral part of the computer generation or they will not move up. Yet it is said that the computer will continue to replace many service and clerical jobs, many of the jobs that women traditionally have held in the large institutions of Western society. How ought one come to terms with the relationship between the employment of one woman who can, with the help of a computer, do the job of many, in relation to the many who are without work because of computer displacement? What effect does the underemployment or unemployment of women have on the partnership of women and men and on their children? Current statistics in the United States show that the single-mother households with children are among the poorest of the poor. What are the alternatives? Is technocracy producing, as one of its human side effects, a more hierarchical class structure among women, as it has already done among men? Is not the solidarity of the women's movement undermined by the very fact that it is educated and privileged women who have the *space* to speak, while silence is still the major "language" of those who are not admitted into the system, those who work for the lowest pay, the longest hours, in the least humanizing employment? Pornography and prostitution symbolize this silence, not making use of women's minds, but reducing women's bodies to objects governed by laws of supply and demand.[8]

TURNING UP THE UNDERSIDE

It is clear that behind the dynamics of women's new consciousness there is a story telling both good and bad news. Some voices express fear that the women's movement, especially in the West, is simply part of the generalized new narcissism—more preoccupation with our own selves as an erotic interest, with our own ego development and self-fulfillment at the expense of getting involved in weightier social, societal issues. In response to this, others counter that, while societal dis-ease can be ignored temporarily, one's own psychological and physical ill-health cannot. Our bodily life and our personal experience are a kind of prism through which we know ourselves in relation to others. Women's own experience, and its imprint on their bodies, is a resource for reflection, knowledge, care, and action about political issues. Women cannot avoid the fact that "the personal is political," that institutional policies and behavior do help, or hinder, women's health.

In the mainstream, women's liberation is a tolerable subject today. Some people, however, are suspicious of the use of the phrase "women's liberation." They fear that this rhetoric is used by those in power as a dodge, as a strategy that in principle opens possibilities for change but that in reality covers up structural issues of dominance and subordination, superiority and inferiority, power and weakness that still buttress male power and shape policy. Those women and men who claim that the liberation of women is the most significant achievement of reform in the twentieth century may be saying one of two things. They may be saying, based on contemporary views of history, that there has been more rapid evolution in the roles and status and attitudes of men toward women and women toward themselves and each other in the twentieth century than in any previous time. Or they may be saying that, compared to other social movements of the twentieth century, the women's movement has had more success in influencing education, law, economics, and political policy in terms of the training of women and the access of women to posts of leadership and policy making.

In examining each of these statements, qualifications need to be made. To the first, one must ask the question, Who writes the history? What is its "underside," as Elise Boulding has begun to explore in her book, *The Underside of History: A View of Women Through Time?*[9] Even in scripture, which is traditionally centered on male leadership and male interpretations of God's engagement in the process of human history, new questions are being asked by women about the social structure of various periods in biblical history, revealing more of the context of women and men's lives, highlighting the traces of women's leadership and of their contributions to daily life—its hazards and joys—as half of the people of God. In the New Testament itself women were the first to discover the empty tomb, the first to witness the risen Christ, the first to tell the news to the men, the ones to open their homes providing meeting places for the first gatherings of the people of the Way, among those listed as apostles and recognized as prophets—these discoveries, added together, portray a dramatically different picture of women and of women/men relationships in the primitive, formative communities of the church. Studies of the developments of later church institutions evidence that women—who were martyrs side by side with the men and often held positions of leadership—were pushed aside as the church became the accepted religion of the Roman Empire and modeled its structures on Roman political and military/hierarchial institutions.[10] Gradually achieving a position of prominence and power, the church adapted to its new station, assuming kingly and military postures, styles, and morals. In the process, women Christians, Christians who were Jewish, Christians without class privileges, were relegated to marginal positions, or they left the church altogether, some becoming part of other religious movements that were critical of the established churches, as Elaine Pagels demonstrates in her book *The Gnostic Gospels.*[11]

BAD NEWS GETS WORSE

On what basis then can we say that the situation for women today is better than it has ever been? It appears to me that it is probably worse, that only for a very elite group of women is the situation globally that much better vis-à-vis the situation of men. As much as one might want, and also need, to isolate women and women's experience in contemporary research, one cannot see a realistic picture of women without viewing the lives of women relative to the lives of men, relative to the societal structure and the social dynamics of the cultures in which both women and men live and die.

Given this perspective I would argue that the situation for women is worse today, because the human situation is worse. Recent historical research has brought to light the pogroms in Europe that preceded the Nazi Holocaust.[12] This provides instruction for us, not only for understanding the seeds of the Holocaust, showing that there were precedents that prepared the way for Adolf Hitler, but also for teaching us how the "civilized" world has dealt violently with racial, ethnic, and religious differences throughout a long history. History is most often written by people who minimize the human costs and brutalities of war—national and civil—because the events are usually recorded by the victors. The heroes (and sometimes heroines) are lifted up, the decisive victories and defeats are remembered in great detail; but there is always the impulse when the war is over to "get on with the peace." No one would criticize the importance of "getting on with the peace," but must this be done by forgetting the war and the root causes that catalyzed it into being? Who wants to remember that more civilians died in World War II than soldiers, that more women, children, handicapped, and elderly were killed than able-bodied military men? Residential bombing, the so-called guerrilla wars of post–World War II and the no partiality atomic bombs, these are also part of the Holocaust, the offering up of unarmed and defenseless citizens, consumed by the fires of Dresden and Hiroshima, as well as by the ovens of Dachau.

What we in the West remember about women during this period is that they entered the work force and took on jobs in the major industries. All reports are that women did a splendid job; then, when the war was over, they were congratulated and sent home. What is only beginning to be documented is that as soon as the peace was declared, women were relived of the "burdens of public work" (working for their country) and returned to the private sphere, to full-time careers of caring for husbands and children. The same women who were considered capable of managing their work and home life during wartime were viewed as no longer capable once the war was over. A more revealing statement might be that jobs were now limited and first priority went to "breadwinners," who were automatically defined as male. Leila Rupp's book, *Mobilizing Women for War*,[13] talks about one side of this phenomenon, and Susan Kennedy's, *If All We Did Was to Weep at Home*,[14] talks about another, the experience of white working women and the fact that they had to keep working because they were chief breadwinners as well. There is nothing wrong with women working full-time at home for their families. In fact, it can be argued that domestic labor is the most important integrating work that humans can do—ordering and creatively caring for the immediate environment in which each of us lives and which we share with others. It is this environment in which we reconstitute our lives and extend them, as a space of hospitality for friends and strangers alike.

Thus, I am not arguing against the full-time homemaker, man or woman. Rather this is a statement against the privatization of the domestic sphere wherein women's or men's lives are narrowed by a withdrawal from responsibility in the public sphere. By not having to face the hassles of work and wages, of company policies and power struggles, large numbers of women become one step removed from where issues are discussed and decisions are made. The picture window to the world becomes a glass barrier. To be "one step removed" has affected women's political attitudes as well. In the post–World II period there was a falling away of women's voluntary organizations previously concerned with larger metropolitan, statewide, and national issues.

Some organizations were an exception; the Women's Strike for Peace, for example, continued to maintain a vigilant eye on international, geopolitical issues, as the League of Women Voters did for state and national concerns. Leaders in the world YWCA also provided a larger vision for local branches as well as a training ground for women in international organizations. Individual leaders saw the need for women in politics and for the perspectives they could bring to issues of peace and human rights. Eleanor Roosevelt envisioned the United States Charter on Human Rights as also a charter for women's human rights, but that vision has still not been internationally accepted. It is still in process, and should become reality; it needs to go yet another step—to be implemented into concrete laws by nation states who hold the ultimate power (politically speaking) over their citizens. With an increasing number of nation states becoming military dictatorships, this does not bode well for the full human rights of anyone, and certainly not for women.

RE-MEMBERING INTO THE FUTURE

Though suppressed, the Holocaust that lies behind us as part of our history also lies ahead of us in re-collection. We *re*-member into the future, whether we wish to or not. Whether or not we wish to assume responsibility for it, it is our inheritance. By not reflecting on the *why* and the *how* of brutal oppression, we deny ourselves the ability to re-collect, to re-orient. Memories of crimes past do not hang dead in the air, but the dynamics shaping the attitudes and the institutional forces that caused them to be committed still function and need to be *re*-membered.[15] That Holocaust has happened does not mean that it cannot happen again; on the contrary it means that it can, will, and even *is* happening not to different people by other means. The act of *re*-membering, of calling to mind again, makes clear the ways in which the personal is structural, the ways in which personal vocational choices involve structural issues, the ways in which work choices are not only a *means* to an end, but are *ends* in themselves. Employees have motives and values they want to perpetuate, and they hire people to accomplish this as well as the specific jobs that need to be done. More and more in ordinary life we are faced with personal decisions that require critical choices between institutional forces that are life-destroying or life-affirming.

TIME AND MONEY

The new sensibilities of women, and of women and men searching for new community, cannot be attributed solely to equality movements, to equal legislation in socialist and semi-socialist nations such as the countries in Scandinavia; nor ought these sensibilities be narrowly focused on the self-awareness, self-knowledge, human potential therapies of women and men in comfortable, affluent sectors of postindustrial culture. Women speaking out is something also intuitional—speaking out from what and for what? The real significance of the women's movement is not yet fully apparent. The apex of the last women's movement in Europe and North America was the mid-1920s, also a time of affluence. It was a dozen years before the Berlin Olympics and the portentous power given to the man who had already published one of the most racist books of our century, *Mein Kampf.* The world we now live in is one that accepts a word produced in the 1950s. That word is *apartheid* (apartness). It is now part of our vocabulary and an assumed part of our international reality. Though we may not want to accept racism as an existing national ideology, we must admit that it is there, acknowledge that a new theory of racial superiority dominates the national life of a major industrial country and a major United States trading partner whose rich mines and black, underpaid miners unearth the gold, uranium, and other precious metals that supply countries and elites that can afford it, East and West, North and South. Black family life is destroyed as a consequence, for wage earners are forced to live separated from their spouses and children for eleven months of the year.

The apex of the last women's movement was a decade before Hitler. One can speculate: How much dialogue existed then between women, Christian and Jew? Might that bridge-building have made a difference? Re-membering into the future, what more might be done to foster community between women, white and black. What actions might be taken in solidarity with the "triumphs and tears" that Hilda Bernstein documents in her work about black women in South Africa?[16]

Today women are crossing global, political, and economic barriers—women in the church, women doing research in cross-cultural anthropology, women in religion, in economic life, in medicine, women engaged in political movements for peace, for justice. There are many more possibilities for women to meet—on their own ground, as women. This is something new. It is made possible by worldwide networks of educated women and by easy means of modern transportation. The airplane has done much to facilitate the revolution of women's consciousness. Provided that money is available and a network of relationships can be established, women today have unique opportunities to meet face-to-face, to be friends, share common issues and organize. Even where this is not possible, books and articles find their way to seemingly impossible, remote places. The fact that educated women around the world speak some English, French, or Spanish, and sometimes German, and are willing to learn other languages, means that the potential for sharing resources and engaging in cross-cultural, cross-national dialogue and networking is greatly enhanced.

THE NEW INTERNATIONALIST

The role of women as new internationalists and its potential cannot be emphasized enough. The United Nations Decade for Women provided occasions for women to meet regularly for the planning of events, to share experiences, to encourage research on women; within the churches there are multiple levels of programming for worldwide women's organizations. Roman Catholic sisters travel and meet together. Networks are developing between associations of sisters as well as among lay Roman Catholic and Protestant women. There are also networks of women in the churches, national and international—Catholic, Protestant, Evangelical, Orthodox—who engage in their own ecumenical conversations, share their own visions, and dialogue with women of other faiths. Choosing their own sacrifices and thanksgivings, these women see each other as women of faith sharing common ground, not primarily as "separated sisters." All this testifies to a new level of life in the ecumenical movement that has its own spirituality and goals. There is evidence of support for one another and of unity in the struggle against continuing to be "the second sex," though Mary Daly's book on the subject is almost twenty years old, and a host of similar works have since followed.[17]

Women, as new internationalists, see with their own eyes, have imprinted on their own experiences, the human tragedies of disease and early death that come to those without regular and relatively easy access to potable water, to food supplies, to shelter from floods, mud, rodents, burning sun and freezing cold. They also see through to the emptiness of insatiable affluence and unmask its power to isolate and self-destruct. Women in various parts of the world have formed communities of solidarity, working with the "invisible" poor in Latin America, organizing women for sobriety in North America, or in West Germany and Switzerland, organizing boycotts against consumer buying of South African fruits purchased for Western markets and family tables at the human price of apartheid. Other women have joined together to research the traffic in sex tourism, in wife buying of Third World brides by Western men. Women in the peace movement continue to cross ideological barriers between the communist and the capitalist spheres of influence, hoping to find common ground and goals and seeking to nurture the possibility of a peaceful global home (private and public) for the next generation. British women in their Greenham Common protest—in refusing to allow their husbands and other male supporters to join them—were declaring that they too want to participate in military decision making. They wanted to present as women a strong profile of protest against the policies of the woman who sits as their head of state.

There is a resolute courage among these women who speak out against human rights violations in their own countries—violations against their sons, their husbands, sometimes their daughters, and even themselves. Often they have themselves been imprisoned and tortured as a consequence. They discover that they are no longer protected against violence because they are women, mothers, young girls, "religious." They find that women are subject to the same harsh, cruel treatment as men prisoners and often to forms of sexual abuse as well. These acts have made many more women politically conscious. Though it has effectively silenced some, it has strengthened many. As one Korean woman has shared, "It has given us strong bones."

Women, as new internationalists, make some national political power elites and their advocates nervous. Though they try at every level to control women, they cannot totally succeed. When a woman's children are threatened, she can call forth an extra measure of raw courage, as evidenced by the Canadian woman who last year rescued her infant from the jaws of a bear by hitting the bear over the head with a frying pan hot off the campfire. Not all stories have such a happy ending, but many match its testimony to self-empowerment and heroism, as in the poetry of Julia Esquivel's *Threatened with Resurrection*.[18]

CONFLICT AND TRANSITION

It is not easy for many women to put themselves in conflict situations. In many cultures, women are the family peacemakers, the reconcilers between various factions. In patriarchal cultures where women are subordinated, they are socialized not to cause conflict; they are trained to stay in the proper place. North American women have had their proper place forcefully pointed out to them by actions such as the lack of passage of the ERA in the United States and by the resistance of the medical profession to women's initiatives to establish their own health clinics—centers informed by "Our Bodies—Ourselves" consciousness that offer women advice and counsel about where and to whom to turn for help, as well as about how to help oneself. About three years ago, the British periodical *New Internationalist* came out with an issue on the apartheid of women—using the terminology on apartheid to analyze women's roles in the economic structures.[19] Among the revealing findings about women were the following:

- They comprise half of the world's people;
- They work two-thirds of the world's working hours;
- They receive one-tenth of the world's income;

- And own only one-hundredth of the world's property;
- Two out of every three illiterate people in the world are women;
- Almost all of the training and technology for improving agriculture is given to men;
- Yet fifty percent of the agricultural production and all of the food processing is the responsibility of women.

It is clear from these facts that there are places where women do not belong; others that are "their proper place." Conflict is inevitable as women begin to claim their half of the total territory.

THE CHURCH

What does this broad sketch of women in transition and transformation have to convey concretely to the churches? Do the influences that affect women throughout the world also affect women in the churches? If this is *not* so, what does it mean for the future of women in the churches? If it *is*, what does it suggest about the churches' chance to change?[20] Are the contributions of women with transformed sensibilities a much needed resource for the renewal of women/men community in the church, or are they regarded as yet another irritant? At this point in history, some people in churches are ambivalent about the new roles of women in the churches—about women's potential influence on shaping ministry, theology, language, worship, and biblical interpretation. While some welcome the changes that will come, others resist. One consequence of this transformed sensibility for congregations is that many potential women leaders—women who might have assumed leadership—have left the churches. They have voted with their feet against the resistance of local congregations and churches to making adaptations that speak not just of how women are different, but about the mutuality of women and men in God's image and that speak of God in images and metaphors that reveal God as encompassing the fullness of humanity, female and male.

Women who have left the churches find it difficult to understand women who have stayed. The dialogue between these two groups is close to nonexistent. Some women leave because it is too painful to stay; others stay because it is too painful to leave.[21] Still others stay because they believe that the church, as the Body of Christ—neither male nor female, rich nor poor, "colored" nor white—has the possibility of renewing itself, has the spiritual and theological foundations to change into a community of genuine partnership, interdependence, and reciprocity, and to establish a full circle of dialogue and communication. These women and men believe the church has the resources with which to create a new community of women, of men, and of women and men; it has the possibility of nurturing the transformation of familial and societal relationships.

There is a commonality among some Christian women who have stayed and some who have left church membership. These women share the same awareness that the church's teachings and theological tradition, its symbols, its interpretations of scripture, have an overwhelmingly patriarchal, male bias. How then is it possible for women to function in such structures? Will they not simply be absorbed, blended in, or kept in a token status? Are new images and models possible?

In the past, women in the church have always been too numerous simply to disappear; accommodations have had to be made. Perhaps this correlates with how woman's differentiated place in the church has developed? In some Christian churches, a strong piety has grown up around Mary. In the Roman Catholic Church this piety has been crystallized into official teaching, with the Assumption of the Virgin Mary. In the Orthodox churches, Mary is *Theodokos,* the Mother God. Her role is at the center of liturgical piety, the Mother of all the living, the bearer of God, of Christ who is one in the divine trinity of God, creator, redeemer, sustainer. Women's roles as separate but equal have been modeled by these powerful patriarchal teachings and liturgical images, images that have generated female symbols to complement the dominating male piety and models for the behavior of the ideal subordinate Christian woman. These projections of male cultural/spiritual power have defined women's place and have located the special place of the feminine. Today many women are aware that they are *not* locked into this projected conceptual destiny, that alternatives exist, that part of women's spirituality is the archeological work of unearthing and re-identifying women's tradition.

The women's movement in the churches has always been related to the education of women. Within current memory this movement is about one-hundred years old. When women were admitted to colleges for the first time, in the days before curricula adjusted to women's needs, women studied Greek, Latin, and Hebrew as did the men. With these linguistic tools, they began to read the Bible in the original languages and thus could uncover the interpretative bias that men interpreters and translators had imposed on scripture. This encouraged them to do their own interpreting, much as people in the Third World do today, working from the languages of the Bible directly to their own mother tongue. In addition, these early feminist women knew that the equal status of women could never be achieved so long as it could be argued on a biblical basis that women are subordinate. They understood very well the power of the Bible over their lives, the power it had, when misused, to legitimize women's subordinated status as it had legitimized slavery. They also saw that it was important for their work to transcend national barriers, so they set up an international committee with representatives from Britain, Scandinavia, and Western Europe to produce the *Woman's Bible*.[22]

At the 1981 meeting of the Society for Biblical Literature, a century after the publication of the *Woman's Bible*, women scholars met to discuss the present status of women's scholarly engagement in biblical interpretation.[23] They made several significant observations. One was that the feminist women who wrote the *Woman's Bible* were not supported by the women scholars who were beginning to teach at that time, mainly at women's colleges, and who were members of the Society for Biblical Literature. By and large, this later group of women did not identify themselves with the religious feminists. Second, they noted that, in 1923, about 9 percent of the membership of the Society for Biblical Literature was women, compared to 3.5 percent in 1981. One of the findings coming again and again from those who research women's history—in a wide variety of male-dominated fields—is (1) that women who have made it into the professions often do not identify with the popular base of the women's movement, and (2) that the participation of women in mainline professions has not steadily grown. There are stops and starts, strong impulses and retreats. Women's engagement in many areas, including biblical scholarship, is an ebb and flow of hopes, disappointments, marginalization in the profession, and separation from other women as part of the cost exacted for some steps forward. The movement of women as a significant force in biblical scholarship is still young. Phyllis Trible's *God and the Rhetoric of Sexuality*[24] is a pioneering work, marking a new frontier of what is still a long journey; Elisabeth Schüssler Fiorenza's *In Memory of Her*[25] has opened up the broad cultural and religious background of the primitive church, revealing the substantial base of women's participation vis-á-vis men's in the Christian community of New Testament times. It is possible that in regard to the new relationships between women and men as a prototype for a new humanity, parallel to "neither Jew nor Gentile, slave nor free," the church we now know is in context, a much backslided version of models in that struggling church of 1900 years ago?

As we look back to re-collect, to gather tradition anew, we are immediately faced with the question of how to appropriate this re-collection in our own time. How is the Word of God addressing us today? This question in turn confronts us with the pressing nearness of the future and with the question of how to appropriate past memory responsibly. Some may ask, Why look back, why remember? It is too painful. Others may say, Why participate in religion at all, with its symbols of patriarchal power? These symbols only add to what is already destructive for women—and for men. Yet still others ask, How can healing take place unless we touch the fire? How can the slave, the prisoner, be free if she/he does not acknowledge the confinement in which she/he lives? Without the re-collecting, acknowledging, acting and reenacting, there can be no envisioning of alternatives, no healing, no reconciliation, no new beginnings. We cannot erase our history; we can only ask that it be forgiven and redeemed and that we be enabled to begin afresh the purifying process of conversion.

Perhaps more than any previous time, this is one for outrageous thoughts—of life and birth and life anew—for we are in a race against time, against death and death fantasies on a scale never known before.[26] Like the yesterdays that must be acknowledged, so also must we acknowledge those signs of a "could-be" tomorrow. Why is it this moment in history, this decade, in which women are emboldened to speak? Is it too much to conjecture that the time of prophecy is returning, that chronologies and calendars must move with the speed of the electronic age if we are still to remember who and whose we are? Are we not vividly reminded today of the pslamist's hope that the God of old is working salvation now in the midst of the earth?

> Thou didst divide the sea by thy might; . . .
> Thou didst crush the heads of Leviathan,
>   thou didst give him as food for the creatures of the wilderness.
>   (Ps. 74:13–14)

In the midst of the glaring inequities and massive forces of destruction, churches—women and men in each local place—are challenged to find the models, means, and audacious intervention points that can foster human life. In many places there are signs of women already so organized: women for peace and against the nuclear arms race; rich and poor women finding common ground on which to defend basic human rights and the quality of familial life; women working for the restoration of the earth, for nurturance of its food-bearing, and for the just distribution of its resources; women across back yards and nations supporting the strengthening of the weak and the weakening of the power-hungry; women reconstituting community life by subverting the powers that divide, neglect, and destroy.

In Israel some years ago, I met a group of Arab and Jewish women who were beginning to come together around the table to eat, to share recipes, to learn something about each other's cooking, households, families, values. For the two groups, living so close to each other yet isolated by the continual threat and presence of war, this cultural sharing was a bold initiative for peace. In searching for a model of the church and its ministry that could be empowered to meet the grave human situation of our time, perhaps the symbol of eating provides a clue, for every

Communion is a re-collecting event, a gathering up of memory, a meal.

For much of church history, Communion has been viewed as a ritual, yet in Christian tradition there is no more forceful symbol of power transformed than the re-membering of Cross and Resurrection at the Meal. It is here that women and men gather without distinction; it is here where they seek forgiveness, repentance, and promise of renewal of life. In facing the reality of the crucified Christ, we gain courage to come face to face with the pain and misery of the Cross in our midst. In participating in the risen Christ, we are invited to venture into an inclusive life as a royal priesthood—royal not just for some, but for all; it is an open invitation for the conversion and participation of all those breaking bread around a common table.

Decisions about the structures and policies in the church influence whether the Meal is seen as reality or ritual. To approach the vision of mutuality in community around a common global table requires sacrifice, a transformation of our prevailing models of authority and power, their access, and use. It was, after all, around the Meal that the first Resurrection communities were created; they were something new. And it was women, previously left out and devoid of power or influence, who were the first to gather and be witnesses to that Resurrection event. As then, so also now, it is not ritualized but *real* events and actions that shape the human course. To re-member our half of the history is not an end in itself, but a fundamental turning point in the re-ordering of a common life for all.

NOTES

INTRODUCTION

1. The classic statement remains Betty Friedan's book, *The Feminine Mystique* (New York: W. W. Norton & Co., 1963). For a strong critique of the early women's movement from the perspective of an ethnic woman, see Bell Hooks, *Ain't I a Woman: Black Women and Feminism* (Boston: South End Press, 1981).
2. For example, see Rosemary Radford Ruether, "Feminism and Peace," *The Christian Century*, August 31, 1983, pp. 771–76. A writer who has focused on ecological issues from a feminist perspective is Elizabeth Dodson Gray, *Green Paradise Lost* (Wellesley, Mass.: Roundtable Press, 1979, 1981).
3. Beverly Wildung Harrison, speech delivered at the Consultation of United Methodist Clergywomen, Dallas, Tex., January 4, 1979.
4. For an excellent description of this process, see Judith Plaskow, "The Coming of Lilith: Toward a Feminist Theology," in *Womanspirit Rising*, ed. Carol P. Christ and Judith Plaskow (San Francisco: Harper & Row, 1979).
5. See Mary Pellauer, "Violence Against Women: The Theological Dimension," *Christianity and Crisis*, May 30, 1983, pp. 206–12.
6. The current focus of controversy is the National Council of Churches booklet *An Inclusive Language Lectionary*, published in 1983 for use in local churches (Atlanta: John Knox Press; New York: The Pilgrim Press; Philadelphia: The Westminster Press).
7. Marjorie Suchocki, "A Servant Office: the Ordination of Women," *Religion in Life*, Summer 1978, p. 197. See also by the same author, "The Unmale God," *Quarterly Review*, Spring 1983, pp. 34–49. A classic analysis of the response of women to the issues of religious language by Diane Tennis is "The Loss of the Father God: Why Women Rage and Grieve," *Christianity and Crisis*, June 8, 1981, pp. 164–70.
8. Daniel Yankelovich, *New Rules: Searching for Self-Fulfillment in a World Turned Upside Down* (New York: Random House, 1981), p. 37.

CHAPTER 1. FEMINIST THEOLOGY AND SPIRITUALITY

1. Mary Wakeman, "Response to Judith Ochshorn," unpublished paper presented at the American Academy of Religion, Greensboro, North Carolina, 1981.

CHAPTER 2. EMERGING ISSUES IN FEMINIST BIBLICAL INTERPRETATION

1. See my "Discipleship and Patriarchy: Early Christian Ethos and Christian Ethics in a Feminist Theological Perspective," in L. Rasmussen, ed., *The Annual of the Society of Christian Ethics* (Waterloo: Wilfried Laurier University, 1982), pp. 131–72. For further development and documentation of the material discussed in this chapter see my book, *In Memory of Her: A Feminist Theological Reconstruction of Christian Origins* (New York: Crossroad, 1983).
2. Redstockings, *New York Manifesto,* 1975.
3. As quoted in Bell Hooks, *Ain't I a Woman: Black Women and Feminism* (Boston: South End Press, 1981) pp. 193f.
4. E. Cady Stanton, *The Original Feminist Attack on the Bible. The Woman's Bible,* intr. by B. Welter, reprint of 1895 ed. (New York: Arno Press, 1974), p. 7.
5. Rosemary Radford Ruether, "Feminism and Patriarchal Religion: Principles of Ideological Critique of the Bible," *Journal for the Study of the Old Testament* 22 (1982), pp. 54–66.
6. "Feminist Critique: Opportunity for Cooperation," ibid., p. 68.
7. See my "'For the Sake of Our Salvation . . .': Biblical Interpretation as Theological Task," in D. Durken, ed., *Sin, Salvation, and the Spirit* (Collegeville, Minn.: The Liturgical Press, 1979), pp. 21–39.
8. Bernadette J. Brooten, "Women Leaders in the Ancient Synagogue," *Brown Judaic Studies* 36 (Chico, Calif.: Scholars Press, 1982).
9. See R. S. Kraemer, "Women in the Religions of the Greco-Roman World," in *Religious Studies Review* 9 (1983), for an extensive discussion of historical-critical studies.
10. See J. B. Metz, *Faith in History and Society: Toward a Practical Fundamental Theology,* trans. D. Smith (New York: Crossroad, 1980).

CHAPTER 3. THE FEMINIST REDEMPTION OF CHRIST

1. Susan Griffin, *Pornography and Silence: Culture's Revenge Against Nature* (New York: Harper & Row, 1981).
2. Mary Condren, in "Patriarchy and Death," a paper delivered at the 1982 American Academy of Religion, shows how the glorification of death and destruction permeates the patriarchal mind, making death the source of life: "Patriarchal birthing takes place primarily through death, the death of defiance of the hero; life-negating spiritualities; the slaughter of the Goddess; the journey into human history by overcoming the fear of death (Hegel), or the murder of the father by the sons (Freud). . . . Nuclear weaponry and destruction is intrinsic to the 'spirituality' generated by Western culture" (pp. 6, 25). Condren's analysis parallels that of Mary Daly: "Patriarchy is itself the prevailing religion of the entire planet, and its essential message is necrophilia" (*Gyn/Ecology: The Metaethics of Radical Feminism* [Boston: Beacon Press, 1978], p. 39).
3. One of the most immobilizing aspects of victimization is the need to be perfect. Anne Wilson Schaef explains that one of the reactions to a deep sense of inferiority is to try to be perfect. *Women's Reality: An Emerging Female System in the White Male System* (Minneapolis: Winston Press, 1981), see especially pp. 28–33, 37–39. Because the smaller subunits of the mass soci-

ety—the family, church, and school—are the arenas in which we feel important as persons, when these interpersonal units mirror the misogynist attitudes of the culture, breaking free to challenge the attitudes is extremely difficult. The source of our sense of worth as persons is also the source of our self-hate. We capitulate to the oppression by trying to be good instead of challenging the misogynist attitudes.

4. Bernard Meland, *Fallible Forms and Symbols* (Philadelphia: Fortress Press, 1976), p. 73.
5. Alice Walker, *The Color Purple* (New York: Harcourt Brace Jovanovich, 1982), pp. 210, 218–19.
6. Meland, p. 73.
7. A pervasive misdefinition of freedom is the notion that freedom is transcendent of context, that freedom is autonomy, self-sufficiency, and independence, a totally internalized subjective self creating itself in an impersonal world. Such notions reflect a concept of a free and transcendent god above and independent of all contingency and the human imitation of the same nonrelational freedom. The existential preoccupation with death is no accident when the definition for freedom is the growing absence of relatedness.
8. Schaef, above, shows that women understand power differently from the white male system (see especially pp. 124–26). Bernard Loomer identifies the ability to make and sustain relationships as "relational power." See "Two Conceptions of Power," *Process Studies* 6:1 (Claremont: Center for Process Studies, 1976), pp. 5–32.
9. Audre Lorde, *Uses of the Erotic: The Erotic As Power* (Brooklyn: Out and Out Books, 1978).
10. Adrienne Rich, *The Dream of a Common Language* (New York: W. W. Norton and Co., Inc., 1978), p. 64.
11. Rich, p. 67.
12. Walker, p. 164.
13. Walker, pp. 166–68.
14. See Barbara Ehrenreich and Deirdre English, *Witches, Midwives, and Nurses: A History of Women Healers* (Old Westbury, N.Y.: The Feminist Press, 1973).
15. George W. Meek in "Toward a General Theory of Healing" from *Healers and the Healing Process*, ed. George W. Meek (Wheaton, Ill.: The Theosophical Publishing House, 1979). After conducting a global study of healing, he believes that healers do not heal. Healers reinforce or supplement a patient's ability to self-heal. Hence, the patient's attitude, the body organism and its energies, and unconscious impulses affect healing possibilities.
16. Doris Lessing, *Canopus in Argos: Archives, Re: Colonized Planet 5 Shikasta* (New York: Vintage Books, 1981).
17. Meland, above, uses the term "mythos" to describe a living structure of meaning. It is "the pattern of meaning and valuations arising from within the structured experience of a people . . . expressing the perceptive truths of the historical experience of a people. . . ." (p. 102).
18. Mary Daly and Mary Condren, cited above, explain that the patriarchal mind involves supplanting birth-giving female images with male cultural creation images, making necessary the killing of the goddess.
19. Tom Driver presents several ethical problems, including sexism and anti-Semitism, as arguments for removing Christ from the Christian center. See *Christ in a Changing World: Toward an Ethical Christology* (New York: Crossroad, 1981).
20. John Berger, *Ways of Seeing* (New York: Penguin Books, 1982), p. 11.

21. Klaus Seybold and Ulrich B. Mueller, *Sickness and Healing* (Nashville: Abingdon, 1981), p. 188.
22. Barbara Ehrenreich and Deirdre English discuss how the emphasis on disorders and cures results in the perpetuation of sexist ideology in the care and treatment of women by the medical profession and how the medical attitude toward women causes disorders. The authors argue for the seizing of the technology of medicine without buying the ideology and for getting women what we need rather than what medicine thinks we should get. See *Complaints and Disorders: The Sexual Politics of Sickness* (Old Westbury, N.Y.: The Feminist Press, 1973), pp. 87, 89.
23. Seybold and Mueller, p. 131.
24. Mary Daly uses this term in *Gyn/Ecology*, pp. 65–67, to describe Dionysus' mother, Semele, who is killed so her son can be born free from Zeus's thigh. She is the ideal of mother as mere vessel who has lost her self.
25. Seybold and Mueller, p. 191.
26. Ibid.
27. Ibid., p. 161.
28. Rich, pp. 64–67.

CHAPTER 4: WOMEN AND MINISTRY: PROBLEM OR POSSIBILITY?

1. An earlier version of this chapter was delivered at the United Presbyterian Church conference, "Celebrate: Women in Ministry," October 24, 1981, Syracuse, New York.
2. J. W. Carroll, B. Hargrove, and A. Lummis, *Women of the Cloth* (San Francisco: Harper & Row, 1983).
3. George Tavard, *Women in Christian Tradition* (Notre Dame: Notre Dame University Press, 1974), p. 219.
4. Constance F. Parvey, ed., *Ordination of Women in Ecumenical Perspective*, Faith and Order paper 105 (Geneva: World Council of Churches, 1980), p. 1.
5. Katherine McAfee Parker, "And Lo! The Time Came . . .," *Concern* 23:1 January 1981, p. 2.
6. Juan Louis Segundo, *The Liberation of Theology* (New York: Orbis, 1976); Carol Christ and Judith Plaskow, eds., *Womanspirit Rising* (San Francisco: Harper & Row, 1979).
7. Thomas S. Kuhn, *The Structure of Scientific Revolutions*, 2nd ed., enlarged (Chicago: University of Chicago Press, 1970), p. 175.
8. Elizabeth Dodson Gray, "Man Above: The Anthropocentric Illusion," *Re-Mything Genesis* (Wellesley, Mass.: Roundtable Press, 1979), pp. 2–8; Chung Choon Kim, "Toward a Christian Theology of Man in Nature," *The Human and the Holy: Asian Perspectives in Christian Theology*, ed. E. Nacpil and D. Elwood (New York: Orbis, 1980), pp. 89–129.
9. Sarah Cunningham, "When in Doubt, Dance," *AD*, June–July 1981, p. 52.
10. Elizabeth H. Verdesi, *In But Still Out: Women in the Church* (Philadelphia: Westminister Press, 1976).
11. Anton Houtepen, "Gospel, Church, Ministry: A Theological Diagnosis of Present Day Problems in the Ministry," *Minister? Pastor? Prophet?* ed. Lucas Grollenberg, et al. (New York: Crossroad, 1981), pp. 22–27.
12. "Study of the Community of Women and Men in the Church: U.S. Section Report," Commission on Faith and Order, National Council of the Churches of Christ, March, 1981.

13. Anton Houtepen, "Koinonia and Consensus: Towards Communion in One Faith," *The Ecumenical Review* 31:1 (January 1979).
14. Parvey, pp. 48–59.
15. James H. Cone, *God of the Oppressed* (New York: Seabury, 1975), p. 15.
16. "Authority-in-Community," drafted by Madeleine Boucher for the Commission on Faith and Order, National Council of the Churches of Christ, March 27–29, 1981. *Mid-Stream* 21:3 (July 1982), pp. 402–17; compare also L. M. Russell, "Women and Unity: Problem or Possibility," pp. 298–304.
17. Dorothee Soelle, *Revolutionary Patience* (New York: Orbis, 1977), p. 16.
18. Frederick H. Borsch, "The Authority of Ministry," *Toward a New Theology of Ordination: Essays on the Ordination of Women*, ed. Marianne H. Micks and Charles P. Price (Richmond: Virginia Theological Seminary, 1976), p. 16.
19. Walter Brueggemann, *The Prophetic Imagination* (Philadelphia: Fortress, 1978), p. 3.
20. Dorothee Soelle, "A Feminist Reflection: Mysticism, Liberation, and the Names of God," *Christianity and Crisis* 41:11 (June 22 1981), p. 183.
21. Lora Gross, "The Embodied Church," in *Women Ministers*, ed. Judith L. Weidman (San Francisco: Harper & Row, 1981), p. 138.
22. Beverly Wildung Harrison, "The Power of Anger in the Work of Love: Christian Ethics for Women and Other Strangers," *Union Seminary Quarterly Review* 37: Supplement (1981), p. 47.
23. Barbara Brown Zikmund, "Women in Ministry Face the '80s," *The Christian Century*, February 3–10, 1982, pp. 113–15.
24. Carroll, Hargrove, Lummis, eds., *Women of the Cloth*, pp. 205–11.
25. Letty M. Russell, "Flight From Ministry," *The Future of Partnership* (Philadelphia: Westminster Press, 1979), chapter 6.
26. Elisabeth Schüssler Fiorenza, "Feminist Theology," *Theological Studies* 36:4 (December 1975), p. 619; see also *Women of Spirit: Female Leadership in the Jewish and Christian Traditions*, ed. Rosemary Radford Ruether and Eleanor McLaughlin (New York: Simon and Schuster, 1979).
27. Elizabeth Dodson Gray, *Patriarchy as a Conceptual Trap* (Wellesley, Mass.: Roundtable Press, 1982), pp. 47–78.
28. Houtepen, "Gospel, Church, Ministry," pp. 32–37.
29. From an interview with Rev. Shannon Clarkson, First Congregational Church of West Haven, Conn., March 1983.
30. Carroll, Hargrove, and Lummis, eds., *Women of the Cloth*, p. 9; E. Wilbur Bock, "The Female Clergy: A Case for Professional Marginality," *American Journal of Sociology* 72 (March 1967), p. 531.
31. Jean Baker Miller, *Toward A New Psychology of Women* (Boston: Beacon Press, 1976), p. 4–9.
32. From an interview with Rev. Shannon Clarkson.
33. Richard Sennett, *Authority* (New York: Vintage Books, 1981), pp. 165–90.
34. Ibid., pp. 175–90.
35. Letty M. Russell, ed., *The Liberating Word: A Guide To Nonsexist Interpretations of the Bible* (Philadelphia: Westminster Press, 1976).

CHAPTER 5. AMERICAN WOMEN AND LIFE-STYLE CHANGE

1. Jessie Bernard, *The Female World* (New York: Free Press, 1981), p. 143.
2. The exception here is women of Asian origin, whose family income as a whole is the highest of any racial group. See U.S. Department of Commerce,

Bureau of the Census, 1980 Census Data in *United States Department of Commerce News*, release dated July 30, 1982.

3. For further information see publications of the Project on the Status and Education of Women of the Association of American Colleges, 1818 R Street, N.W., Washington, D.C. 20009.

4. Susan Brownmiller observes that the fear of rape or bodily harm keeps all women in a state of subordination. See *Against Our Will: Men, Women, and Rape* (New York: Simon and Schuster, 1975).

5. Paul Glick, "The Future of the American Family," U.S. Department of Commerce, Current Population Reports, Special Series, Series P–23, no. 78 (Washington, D.C.: Government Printing Office, 1979), pp. 1–5.

6. Ibid., p. 4.

7. The 1980 Census found about 3.8 million cohabiting persons, about 3 percent of the population.

8. Present projections suggest that about 10 percent of all persons will never marry, a figure about equal to that during the Great Depression.

9. Glick, pp. 34.

10. Ibid., p. 4.

11. Ibid., p. 5.

12. "Portrait of America," *Newsweek*, January 17, 1983, p. 26.

13. Jessie Bernard, *The Future of Marriage* (New Haven & London: Yale University Press, rev. 1982), pp. 3–76.

14. I. Broverman, et al., "Sex-role Stereotypes and Clinical Judgments of Mental Health," *Journal of Consulting and Clinical Psychology*, 24:1–7, 1970.

15. Karen Horney, *Feminine Psychology* (New York: W. W. Norton and Co., Inc., 1967), passim, but especially "The Problem of Feminine Masochism," pp. 214ff.

16. See for example Elizabeth Janeway, *Man's World, Woman's Place* (New York: Dell, 1971), especially chapter 4, pp. 48–58.

17. *Newsweek*, p. 27.

18. For a careful study of the acculturation of young girls, see Caryl Rivers, et al., *Beyond Sugar and Spice* (New York: G. Putnam and Sons, 1979).

19. For black women, the comparison with the income of males is fifty-four cents to the dollar; for Hispanics, forty-nine cents to the dollar. See "Population Facts on Women of Color," from the National Institute for Women of Color, 1712 N Street, N.W., Washington, D.C. 20036.

20. *Newsweek*, p. 27.

21. Judith S. Wallerstein and Joan Kelly, "California's Children of Divorce," *Psychology Today*, January 1980, pp. 67–76.

22. "Child Support and Alimony," U.S. Department of Commerce, Current Population Reports, Special Series, Series P–23, no. 106 (Washington, D.C.: Government Printing Office, 1978).

23. *National NOW Times*, October 1982, p. 2.

24. *New York Times*, May 24, 1982, sec. A, p. 17.

25. "American Families and Living Arrangements," U.S. Department of Commerce, Current Population Reports, Special Series P–23, no. 104 (Washington, D.C.: Government Printing Office, 1980), p. 10.

26. Bernard, *The Female World*, p. 156.

27. Rochelle Semmel Albin, reporting on studies by Dr. Grace Baruch, et al., in "Has Feminism Aided Mental Health?" *New York Times*, June 16, 1981, sec. C.

28. See "The Gray Paper, Shared Housing," *Ms*, January, 1982, pp. 83–86.

29. Nancy Loving, "Spouse Abuse: The Hidden Crime," *engage/social action* 10:3 (March 1982), p. 24.

30. *Newsweek*, p. 27.
31. National Council on Economic Opportunity Report, quoted in *Ms*, January 1982, p. 37.
32. See "Fact Sheet on Women: Women and Aging," published by the American Council of Life Insurance and the Health Insurance Association of America, 1850 K Street, N.W., Washington, D.C. 20006, Fall; 1982.
33. *Newsweek*, pp. 30–31.
34. See "Trends in Child Care Arrangements of Working Mothers," U.S. Department of Commerce, Current Population Reports, Special Series, Series P-23, no. 117 (Washington, D.C.: Government Printing Office, 1982).
35. Linda J. Waite, *U.S. Women at Work* 36:2 (May 1981), Population Reference Bureau, Inc., pp. 10ff.
36. *Newsweek*, p. 33.
37. For an incisive analysis of the links between the patriarchal family and the economic system, see Zellah R. Eisenstein, "The Sexual Politics of the New Right: Understanding the 'Crisis of Liberalism' for the 1980s," *Signs*, 7:3 (Spring 1982), pp. 567–88.
38. Bernard, *The Future of Marriage*, p. 289.
39. Adrienne Rich, "From an Old House in America," in *Adrienne Rich's Poetry*, ed. Barbara Charlesworth Gelpi and Albert Gelpi (New York: W. W. Norton & Co., Inc., 1975), p. 85.

CHAPTER 6. LIBERATING WORK

1. I would like to express my gratitude to the members of the Berkeley Women and Work Study group who have met together for the past year and a half. My sisters in study have provided support of and helpful criticism toward the construction of a feminist theology of work.
2. Anna Pawelczynska, *Values and Violence in Auschwitz* (Berkeley: University of California Press, 1979).
3. Gregory Baum, *The Priority of Labor* (New York: Paulist Press, 1982).
4. Harry Braverman, *Labor and Monopoly Capital* (New York: Monthly Review Press, 1974), especially part IV; also, Jean Tepperman, *Not Servants, Not Machines; Office Workers Speak Out* (Boston: Beacon Press, 1976).
5. See Elise Boulding, *The Underside of History* (Boulder, Colo.: Westview Press, 1976) for a pioneer study of women's historical contribution to material and cultural life.
6. The poem appeared in M. K. Raj and V. Patel, "Women's Liberation and the Political Economy of Housework: An Indian Perspective," *Women's Studies International* 2 (July 1982), p. 16.
7. See, for example, "Women in the Workplace," *Signs* 1(3) (Spring 1976); "The Labor of Women: Work and the Family," *Signs* 4(4) (Summer 1979); "Workers, Reproductive Hazards, and the Politics of Protection," *Feminist Studies* 5(2) (Summer 1979); "Women and Work," *Feminist Studies* 8:2 (Summer 1982).
8. Isabel Carter Heyward, *The Redemption of God* (Washington, D.C.: University Press of America, 1982).
9. *Work, Society, and Culture* (New York: Fordham University Press, 1971), p. 1.
10. Hannah Arendt, *The Human Condition* (Chicago: University of Chicago Press, 1958).
11. Among such studies: Georges Friedmann, *The Anatomy of Work* (New York: The Free Press, 1961); Barbara Garson, *All the Livelong Day* (New York:

Doubleday & Co., 1975); Robert Schrank, *Ten Thousand Working Days* (Cambridge: MIT Press, 1978).

12. Studs Terkel, *Working* (New York: Pantheon Press, 1974).
13. Peter Lengyel, ed., "Work," *International Society Science Journal* 32 (1980).
14. Kathleen Newland, *Women, Men and the Division of Labor* (Washington, D.C.: Worldwide Institute, 1980).
15. Ester Boserup, *Women's Role in Economic Development* (London: George Allen & Unwin, 1970); Nici Nelson, *Why Has Development Neglected Rural Women?* (Oxford: Pergamon Press, 1979).
16. Baum; see appendix, which contains full text of the encyclical.
17. Maria Reiley, O.P., "Women Workers in the Global Factory," *Center Focus*, January 1983, p. 2.
18. Baum, p. 79.
19. Data derived from the reports of the National Commission on Working Women, which incorporate the U.S. Labor Department estimates for 1980.
20. Newland, p. 11.
21. Rosalind Petchesky, "Workers, Reproductive Hazards, and the Politics of Protection," *Feminist Studies* 5:2 (Summer 1979), p. 235.
22. Peggy Sanday, *Female Power and Male Dominance* (Cambridge: Cambridge University Press, 1981), p. 76.
23. See, for example, Michelle Z. Rosaldo and Louise Lamphere, eds., *Women, Culture, and Society* (Stanford: Stanford University Press, 1974), passim.
24. Sherry Ortner, "Is Female to Male as Nature Is to Culture?" in Rosaldo and Lamphere, pp. 67–88.
25. Sanday, p. 90.
26. See Frances Dahlberg, ed., *Woman, the Gatherer* (New Haven: Yale University Press, 1981), passim.
27. Carol MacCormack, "Nature, Culture, and Gender: A Critique," in Carol MacCormack and Marilyn Strathern, eds., *Nature, Culture, and Gender* (London: Cambridge University Press, 1980), p. 6.
28. Susan Griffin, *Women and Nature* (New York: Harper & Row, 1978) and *Pornography and Silence* (New York: Harper & Row, 1981).
29. Rachel Grossman, "Women's Place in the Integrated Circuit," *Radical America* 14:2 (January/February 1980), pp. 29–49.
30. Reiley, p. 3.
31. Naomi Katz and D. S. Kemnitzer, "Fast Forward: The Internationalization of Silicon Valley," in June Nash and Patricia Fernandez, eds., *Women, Men, and the International Division of Labor* (New York: SUNY Press, 1983).
32. Katz and Kemnitzer estimate that almost half of the women production workes have come from Southeast Asia, the Phillipines, and Tonga.
33. Clare B. Fischer, "The Fiery Bridge: Simone Weil's Theology of Work," Dissertation, Graduate Theological Union, 1979; Weil kept a journal of her experiences that remains untranslated from the original French (*La condition ouvrière*, 1951).
34. See Fischer, chapter 2, for discussion of Weil's work reform.
35. See Simone Weil, "Factory Work," in George Panichas, ed., *The Simone Weil Reader* (New York: David McKay Co., Inc., 1977), pp. 53–72.
36. I am indebted to Craig Moro, who in conversation used "re-member" in its usual sense of recalling and as a symbol of healing that which is dismembered.
37. Newland, p. 25.
38. Barbara Epstein, "Industrialization and Femininity: A Case Study of Nineteenth-Century New England," in Rachel Kahn-Hut, A. K. Daniels, R. Col-

vard, eds., *Women and Work* (New York: Oxford University Press, 1982), pp. 88–100.

39. Epstein, p. 95.
40. Martha May, "The Historical Problem of the Family Wage: The Ford Motor Company and the Five Dollar Day," *Feminist Studies* 8:2 (Summer 1982), pp. 399–424.
41. Newland, pp. 21–24; she reports on the University of Michigan's survey findings that indicate little change in actual hours per week spent in "family care" between 1965 and 1975.
42. See M. K. Raj and V. Patel, who indicate that Indian women spend almost nine years of fifty in kitchen work.
43. Joann Vanek, "Time Spent in Housework," in Alice Amsden, ed., *The Economics of Women and Men* (New York: St. Martin's Press, 1980), pp. 82–90.
44. Nona Y. Glazer, *The Invisible Intersection: Involuntary Unpaid Labor Outside the Household and Women Workers* (Berkeley: The Center for the Study, Education, and Advancement of Women, University of California, 1982).
45. Glazer, pp. 39–40.
46. Charlotte Perkins Gilman, *Women and Economics* (Boston, 1898; New York: Harper & Row, 1966).
47. Judith Barwick, *Women in Transition* (Sussex: Harvester Press, 1980), p. 41.
48. "Women in the Workplace," *Signs* 1:3 (Spring 1976).
49. Teresa Marciano, "Socialization and Women at Work," *National Forum* 59:4, pp. 24–25; see Maresi Nerad, "Hidden Functions of Higher Education: The Perpetuation of Women's Domestic Work and the Professionalization of Women's Work in the Labor Market," Berkeley, 1983 (unpublished manuscript).
50. Nancy Barrett, "Women in the Job Market: Occupations, Earnings, and Career Opportunities," in Ralph Smith, ed., *The Subtle Revolution—Women at Work* (Washington, D.C.: The Urban Institute, 1979), p. 46.
51. Ruth Friedman, "Desex Schooling for Jobs," *New York Times* (March 6, 1983).
52. Peter Kerr, "Woman's Work: Rarely Blue Collar," *New York Times* (July 14, 1982).
53. Ruth Milkman, "Redefining 'Woman's Work': The Sexual Division of Labor in the Auto Industry During World War II," *Feminist Studies* 8:2 (Summer 1982), pp. 337–72.
54. Ellen Lewin, "Feminist Ideology and the Meaning of Work: The Case of Nursing," *Catalyst* nos. 10–11 (Summer 1977), pp. 78–103.
55. Carolina Maria deJesus, *Child of the Dark* (New York: E. P. Dutton & Co., 1962).
56. deJesus, p. 57.
57. Harriet Arnow, *The Dollmaker* (New York: Avon, 1971).
58. Ibid., p. 599.
59. Pawelczynska, p. 15.
60. June Nash, *We Eat the Mines and the Mines Eat Us* (New York: Columbia University Press, 1979), p. 16.

CHAPTER 7. HUMAN SEXUALITY AND MUTUALITY

1. This chapter was first delivered at a symposium on October 21–22, 1982, at Princeton Theological Seminary to mark the fifteenth anniversary of the adoption of the Confession of 1967 of the United Presbyterian Church. It is

adapted from the *Journal of Presbyterian History* (Spring 1983) and used by permission.

2. Samuel Laeuchli, *Power and Sexuality* (Philadelphia: Temple University Press, 1972), p. 92.

3. James Nelson, *Embodiment: An Approach to Sexuality and Christian Theology* (Minneapolis: Augsburg Press, 1979).

4. *Jerome*, Letter 22:25–6 and *Against Jovinian* 1:9, 16, 26–31. See also: J. N. D. Kelly, *Jerome, His Life, Writings and Controversies* Westminster, Md.: Christian Classics, Inc., 1980.

5. Nancy Jay, "Throughout Your Generations Forever: A Sociology of Blood Sacrifice," Ph.D. diss., Brandeis University, 1981.

6. H. R. Trevor-Roper, *The Great Witch Craze of the Sixteenth and Seventeenth Centuries and Other Essays* (New York: Harper Torchbooks, 1967).

7. Compare Emil Brunner, *Man in Revolt: A Christian Anthropology* (Philadelphia: Westminster Press, 1947), see especially p. 352*f.*; Karl Barth, *The Church Dogmatics*, ed. G. W. Bromily and T. F. Torrance, vol. III:4 (Edinburgh: T. T. Clark, 1961), pp. 116–240.

8. Boston Women's Health Collective, *Our Bodies, Ourselves* (New York: Simon & Schuster, 1973).

9. John MacMurray, *The Self as Agent* (London: Farber & Farber, 1958); *Persons in Relation* (London: Faber & Farber, Limited, 1961).

10. Isabel Carter Heyward, *The Redemption of God: A Theology of Mutual Relation* (Washington, D.C.: University Press of America, 1982), p. 25f.

11. Nelle Morton, "The Rising Consciousness of Women in a Male Language Structure," *Andover-Newton Quarterly* 12:4, (March 1972).

12. Michael Lewis, *The Culture of Inequality* (Amherst: University of Massachusetts Press, 1979), chap. 1.

13. William Ryan, *Blaming the Victim* (New York: Random House, 1971).

14. See Johnny Greene, "The Moral Wrongs of the New Moral Right," *Playboy*, January 1981.

15. Gustavo Gutierrez, *A Theology of Human Liberation* (Maryknoll, Orbis Books, 1973).

16. Dorothee Soelle, *Beyond Mere Obedience* (Philadelphia: Fortress Press, 1981).

CHAPTER 8. RE-MEMBERING: A GLOBAL PERSPECTIVE ON WOMEN

1. The word *holos* in Greek points to that which is whole, entire, complete, not divided and disjointed, sound and healthy; contemporary use of the word *wholeness* comes from this Greek root.

2. *Almanac for Women: About Women*, no. 1 (London: Sheba Feminist Publications, September 1980; first printed December 10 1979).

3. H. G. Shaffer, *Women in the Two Germanies* (Elmsferd: Pergamon Press, 1981).

4. *Rural Women's Participation in Development*, Evaluation Study no. 3, United Nations Development Programme, New York, June 1980.

5. World Military and Social Expenditures, 1981. *Development: Seeds of Change*, 1982. In the same issue, see Inga Thorsson, "The Arms Race and Development: A Competitive Relationship," which describes how "steadily high or increasing military outlays tend to depress economic growth."

6. *Newsweek*, January 24, 1983, p. 9.

7. *Credit and Women's Economic Development*, World Council of Credit Unions,

Inc., in collaboration with Overseas Education Fund, Washington, D.C., 1981.

8. Laura Lederer, ed., *Take Back the Night* (New York: Morrow, 1980). See also Susan Griffin's *Pornography and Silence* (New York: Harper & Row, 1982).

9. Elise Boulding, *The Underside of History: A View of Women Through Time* (Boulder, Colo.: Westview Press, 1976).

10. K. Thraede and G. Scharfenorth, *Freunde in Christus Werden*, vol. 1 (*Frauen als Innovationsgruppen*) (Gelnhausen: Burckhardthaus-Laetare Verlag, 1978).

11. Elaine Pagels, *The Gnostic Gospels* (New York: Vintage Books Edition, 1981).

12. Yosef Hayim Yerushalmi, *The Lisbon Massacre of 1506 and the Royal Image of Shebete Yehudah* (Cincinnati: Hebrew Union College, Jewish Institute of Religion, 1976). See also his earlier work on *The Inquisition and the Jews in France at the Time of Bernard Gui* (Rutgers Hebraic Studies, vol. 1, 1965).

13. Leila Rupp, *Mobilizing Women for War* (Princeton, N.J.: Princeton University Press, 1978.

14. Susan S. Kennedy, *If All We Did Was to Weep At Home: A History of White Working-Class Women In America* (Bloomington: Indiana University Press, 1979).

15. George M. Kren, and L. Rappoport, *The Holocaust and the Crisis of Human Behavior* (New York: Holmes and Meir, 1980). See particularly chapter 1, "Dimensions of the Historical Crisis."

16. Hilda Bernstein, *For Their Triumphs and for Their Tears: Women in Apartheid South Africa* (London: International Defense and Aid Fund, May 1978).

17. Mary Daly, *The Church and the Second Sex: With a New Feminist Post-Script* (New York: Harper & Row, 1975).

18. Julia Esquivel, *Threatening with Resurrection* (Elgin, Ill.: The Brethren Press, 1982).

19. Leslie Adamson, ed., "More to Lose Than Their Chains," *New Internationalist* no. 89 (July 1980), pp. 7–11. See the "World's Women Data Sheet" published by the Population Reference Bureau, Washington, D.C., in collaboration with UNICEF.

20. Betty Thompson, *A Chance to Change* (Philadelphia: Fortress, 1982).

21. Sara Maitland, *A Map of the New Country: Women and Christianity* (London and Boston: Routledge and Kegan Paul, 1983).

22. Elizabeth C. Stanton, *Woman's Bible* (1895; Seattle: Coalition on Women and Religion, 1974).

23. *Journal for the Study of the Old Testament* 22 (February 1982).

24. Phyllis Trible, *God and the Rhetoric of Sexuality* (Philadelphia: Fortress, 1978).

25. Elisabeth Schüssler Fiorenza, *In Memory of Her* (New York: Crossroad, 1983).

26. Stockholm International Peace Research Institute, *World Armaments and Disarmament Yearbook, 1982* (Cambridge, Mass.: Oelgeschlager, Gunn, and Hain, 1983).

Index